MOZART WIND AND STRING CONCERTOS

BBC MUSIC GUIDES

Mozart Wind and String Concertos

A. HYATT KING

BRITISH BROADCASTING CORPORATION

Published by the British Broadcasting Corporation
35 Marylebone High Street, London W1M 4AA

ISBN 0 563 12770 8

First published 1978

© A. Hyatt King 1978

Printed in England by The Whitefriars Press Ltd,
London and Tonbridge

Contents

The two passages from Schachtner's letter to Mozart's sister are quoted from *Mozart. A documentary biography*, by Otto Erich Deutsch, translated by Eric Blom, Peter Branscombe and Jeremy Noble (A. & C. Black, 1966). All passages cited from other letters are from the second edition of *The Letters of Mozart and his Family*, translated and edited by Emily Anderson (Macmillan, 1966).

Introduction

Mozart has been described as the prince of concerto composers. His earliest music in this form (not original works, it is true) dates from 1767, his eleventh year: he finished his last concerto only some seven or eight weeks before he died. In the intervening twenty-five years, he composed over fifty concertos, and began half a dozen or so more which he left uncompleted. The most numerous group comprises, of course, those for piano, which have a unique position in his creative life. For of all his instrumental works they offer the best material for studying the steady development of his mature style. The concertos that he composed from the winter of 1782 onwards were mostly intended for his own performance, as the means of keeping his name before the Viennese public. In these and other respects the piano concertos offer a strong contrast to those for stringed and wind instruments – the 'miscellaneous' concertos which are the subject of this BBC Music Guide.

One of the chief reasons for this contrast lies in a difference of chronological pattern dictated by circumstances. During Mozart's adolescence in Salzburg and his later European journeys, he met a fairly steady demand for 'miscellaneous' concertos. This went on for nearly fifteen years, until the early 1780s. After he settled in Vienna, the piano became all-pervasive, opera made increasing demands on his time and energy, and the subtleties of chamber music provided a more and more engrossing attraction as the medium for his most intimate thoughts and feelings. Even if Mozart had then received numerous requests for 'miscellaneous' concertos, he would hardly have had time to satisfy them. In fact, between 1784 and 1790 the only instrument, apart from the piano, for which he wrote a sequence of concertos was the horn.

Again, though the 'miscellaneous' concertos fall into several groups none of which was very numerous except the concertos for violin, and to a lesser extent for the horn, no single group extended over a period long enough for Mozart to develop his style effectively within it. This discontinuity may have been due partly to the fact that, besides the piano, Mozart himself played only the viola and violin, and, as far as we know, only the latter in public. In consequence, however eagerly he responded to the stimulus of travel and the requests it brought from soloists or groups of players, the impetus for the 'miscellaneous' concertos remained largely external.

The general result was therefore spasmodic and rather haphazard.

A number of the 'miscellaneous' concertos also differ from those for piano because they pose problems of authenticity, text and date. The cause of this may be traced partly, again, to chronology, and partly to Mozart's own habits. Unsystematic as he was in some ways, he seems after his marriage to have made an effort to keep track of his music. One visible sign is the thematic catalogue which he began in February 1784. His good intentions can also be seen in the quantity of autograph scores which he preserved as he grew older, and which he left to his widow. She ultimately sold the bulk of them to the Offenbach publisher J. A. André, and in time a good many found their way into institutional libraries. In this way, most of the autographs of the piano concertos have been preserved. But those of the 'miscellaneous' concertos, having been mostly written before 1784, fared far less well.

Some of these autograph scores Mozart probably gave away to the soloist or patron, and their conservation thus became much more a matter of chance. Consequently, the autographs of some very important works probably vanished before Mozart's death and have never been seen since. The alternative sources are of questionable value. Thus, besides having an unsatisfactory text, we do not know whether certain concertos are entirely genuine or at what date they were composed. There are other uncertainties as well which admittedly even the autograph would probably not have reduced, such as the occasion of the first performance or the identity of the soloist for whom the work was intended. While such uncertainties seldom affect the piano concertos (partly because the autographs are extant and partly because their focus is largely Mozart himself), they are relevant, in some cases vitally so, to our understanding of some of the 'miscellaneous' concertos.

Their musical quality is variable. There are none that scale heights such as those of the olympian Piano Concerto in C (K503), or plumb depths comparable to those of the C minor. But in Mozart there are many varieties of excellence, and the sequence of those 'miscellaneous' concertos, taken as a whole, contains much marvellous music. We have masterpieces such as the powerful Sinfonia Concertante (K364/320d)[1], the lyrical Clarinet Concerto, and, on a lower plane, the Flute Concerto in G and the last two horn

[1] Where two Köchel numbers are given, the second is that in the sixth edition of Köchel (Wiesbaden 1964).

8

concertos, all perfect of their kind. Moreover, since Mozart had the opportunity to compose a solo work or music in concerto style for nearly every instrument in the normal concert orchestra of his time, the range of sonorities alone is a source of endless delight.

So, in this field, Mozart is revealed as a masterly opportunist, in the best sense of the word, meeting each challenge as it came. He lavished on these concertos all the poetic wealth of his genius. In many of them, technical ingenuity blends happily with outstanding economy of means. Besides their musical fascination, some of these concertos are rich in a variety of historical and personal interest. For the letters of Mozart and his father and other documents tell us something about their place in the concert life of the time. The composer himself introduces us to some of his patrons and, above all, to the players for whom he wrote this delectable music.

We can now consider the concertos in detail. They fall conveniently into several groups which correspond more or less to the chronological sequence of composition. First come a few early works, including the popular Bassoon Concerto (K191), followed by the violin concertos. Five of these date from 1775, and there are also a handful of related single movements. To all these we may add three other violin concertos which pose problems of date or authenticity in various degrees. From the years 1778 to 1780 we have the works for flute and oboe. The remarkable compositions in concertante style all date from roughly the same period. Then come the concertos and single movements for horn, which were spread over some five years, the majority written between 1781 and 1783, followed by the last concerto, an isolated work of 1786. Finally we have the incomparable Clarinet Concerto of 1791. To round off the whole picture a few lost works and some important fragmentary concertos also deserve brief mention.

Juvenilia

Mozart's earliest concertos were the four for harpsichord (K37, 39–41), dating from the spring and summer of 1767. But since they consist of movements orchestrated (with his father's help) from keyboard sonatas of various contemporary composers, they cannot

be ranked as original in any sense. It is therefore all the more unfortunate that what was most probably Mozart's earliest original
concerto, the work for trumpet (K47c) composed late in 1768, is
now lost. Nevertheless, its purpose and the circumstances of its
performance are so exceptional that they merit description at some
length. Here we have the first example of a concerto which Mozart
wrote to fulfil a commission.

In September 1767 the Mozarts began their second sojourn in
Vienna during which they expected to participate actively in the
musical festivities connected with the intended marriage of the
Archduchess Maria Josepha and King Ferdinand of Naples. But the
Archduchess died in October, and consequently much public music-
making was suspended, to the dismay of the Mozarts who en-
countered many obstacles and lingered until early in January 1769.
The boy's principal works during this time were two operas,
Bastien und Bastienne and *La finta semplice*, six symphonies, and some
church music. Of the last, by far the most extensive commission
came from the newly-built Waisenhaus-Kirche (the Orphanage
Church) in the Rennweg. Ignaz Parhamer, its director, was a
friend of the Mozart family and asked the boy to compose music for
the service of consecration which took place, in the presence of
Maria Theresa, four of her children, and the Archbishop of Vienna,
on 7 December 1768. Mozart composed a Solemn Mass, an Offer-
tory, and a trumpet concerto, all of which he conducted himself.
Leopold tells us that the concerto was played by a boy, presumably
one of the large musical establishment in the orphanage. However
unusual it may seem today, such concertos were regularly played
at High Mass in Viennese churches during the Gradual.

It is perhaps rather hazardous to have described this concerto as
'original', in the light of the share which we know Leopold Mozart
had in some of his son's early music. Moreover, as Leopold had
himself composed a trumpet concerto in 1762, he was well qualified
to give technical advice. On the other hand, the nature of the music,
the occasion, and the comparative rarity of such concertos, make it
probable that this work was original, however much the boy was
guided by his father and perhaps influenced (as later in his life) by
Michael Haydn, whose trumpet concerto comes from 1763 or
1764. We know that Mozart's work was played several times in the
years immediately after 1768, and our knowledge of the first
performance brings vividly to life this episode in his childhood. It

is also curious that the boy should have composed his first concerto for the one instrument which, until three years before, simply terrified him. Schachtner, the Salzburg court trumpeter and a close friend of the Mozart family, wrote:

Until he was almost 9 he was terribly afraid of the trumpet when it was blown alone, without other music. Merely to hold a trumpet in front of him was like aiming a loaded pistol at his heart. Papa wanted to cure him of this childish fear and once told me to blow [my trumpet] at him despite his reluctance, but my God! I should not have been persuaded to do it; Wolfgangerl scarcely heard the blaring sound, than he grew pale and began to collapse, and if I had continued, he would surely have had a fit.

In the five years from 1768 to 1773 Mozart's genius developed with astonishing rapidity. He composed over 130 works – church music, operas, arias, songs, symphonies, serenades, divertimenti and chamber music. But he wrote few piano works, and even fewer concertos. Such paucity may be partly explained by the fact that during this time he spent nearly two and a half years away from home, two of them in Italy where the demand for concertos seems to have been limited. But one might have expected that in Salzburg or in Vienna (where Mozart spent nearly four months) there would have been some occasion for a player to ask him for a new work. As it was, however, only twice in these five years did he write concertos, each time in Salzburg, and for himself as a harpsichordist. The first work dates from about 1771, when, as in 1767, he again arranged music by another composer, namely J. C. Bach, three of whose sonatas Op. 5 he scored as concertos with string accompaniment (K107). The second concerto was the brilliant, aggressive and often most original work in D (K175, 1773) which was a landmark in his career and which he retained successfully in his concert repertory for some time.

But the demand for other such music, though slow at first, increased steadily. It began in the spring of 1774, when Mozart seems to have received two commissions in quick succession. This at least is the implication of the date on the autographs. The first work was the Concertone in C for two Violins (K190/186E) which Mozart dated 31 May 1774. (Someone later crossed out the date with such a heavy stroke that it became partially illegible and, until a few years ago, was misread as 3 May 1773.) The second concerto is that for bassoon, in F (K191/186e), which he dated 4 June 1774. Thus only three days separate the completion of the two works.

The 'Concertone for two Violins' (as it is generally described, though Mozart wrote only 'Concertone' on the autograph) is true to its Italian title. For it shows strong Italian influences and, although composed over a year after he returned from Italy, recalls the free treatment of solo instruments found in the Divertimento in E flat, K113, written in Milan in November 1771. K190 is a hybrid work, in which an older style is wedded to a new spirit; the contrasting groups of the baroque concerto grosso, as developed by Corelli and Tartini, blend happily with the smoother melodic line and the calculated elegance of the *style galant*. This concertone is in fact a concertante piece, in which, besides the two solo violins, the oboe is frequently prominent, and the cello as well has an occasional share of glory. Although half a dozen or so of Mozart's near-contemporaries composed concertones, none seem to have survived. At least we know his was not an isolated work, but part of a limited yet significant tradition. We can see clear traces of it in Joseph Haydn's symphonies nos. 6, 7 and 8 which Mozart may have heard when he was in Vienna in 1773.

Besides being rather old-fashioned historically, this Concertone marks a somewhat static point in his development. Compared with the assertive, thrusting style of the Harpsichord Concerto in D, completed only a few months before, the concertone lacks, through its very nature, dramatic tension and any marked sense of formal purpose. But the scoring is bright and fairly powerful, for oboes, horns, trumpets (omitted in the second movement), and a full complement of strings. Mozart, now well into his nineteenth year, adds occasional variety of colour from divided violas, and by separating the cellos from the contrabass. He was rapidly learning to exploit orchestral resources, and doubtless missed the clarinets available in Milan for the above-mentioned Divertimento K113.

The first movement of the Concertone, marked 'allegro spiritoso', is spaciously constructed, with abundant melodic interest. The bold unisons of the opening tutti make an effective contrast to the first concertante statement, where the violins enter in canon, followed by the oboe – a pattern followed closely throughout this movement and the finale. At the beginning of the development, however, Mozart draws the same three soloists together in the dominant, to announce a new theme, enriched by cello and bass playing solo – the sort of sharp contrast for which his instinct was unerring. In the recapitulation he springs a little surprise by shortening the opening tutti from nineteen bars to four, and then plunges straight into the canonic solo entry. He rounds off the movement with a pretty cadenza for violins and oboe.

At 192 bars, the 'andante grazioso' (in F) is exceptionally long, perhaps too much so for the rather slender emotional content. But despite this and a limited sense of tonal adventure, the music has charm and delicacy, enhanced by much precision in dynamic markings and by some purling chromaticism akin to the style of Michael Haydn. Mozart also displays some structural ingenuity. We never quite know which theme will appear next; for instance, the first solo entry alternates effectively with unexpected interjections from the opening tutti. He deploys the concertante style in various ways, notably by giving the cello an extensive part, and by allowing oboe and cello to steal the show in triplets at the end of the exposition. For them and the violin he writes another engaging cadenza, of some eighteen bars.

The third movement marks a return to the open texture of the first, within the framework of a loose-limbed, rambling minuet of the kind much favoured in Northern Italy during the 1770s. So Mozart reverts to the style of some of the quartets he wrote in Milan in 1772. Though we may feel that the minuet-finale of the concertante is rather superficial in tone, it is undeniable that Mozart lavished much pains upon it. His attention to detail softens the rather hard, formal outlines. In the quieter sections which alternate with the bustling passage work, he sometimes uses expression marks very carefully – *dolce* shading off gradually to *pp*. The solo instruments enjoy themselves most in the trio-section, where the violins and oboe play florid passages *alternatim*, and then give way to the cello. Here, too, we find an effective blend of oboes and horns alternating with the solo strings supported by divided violas and trumpets. It is Mozart's handling of orchestral colour which gives this rather formal music its character and, indeed, a touch of richness here and there.

We know nothing of the occasion for which Mozart composed the concertone. It seems likely that he intended it for the court orchestra, perhaps on some festal occasion, or for an informal band such as could readily be assembled in Salzburg from amateurs with professional strengthening. The soloists might all have been drawn from the Archbishop's players. In the court calendars of about this time the two senior violinists are named as Wenzl Sadlo and Joseph

Hülber, the solo cellist was J. A. Marschall, and the two oboists were Franz de Paula Deibl and Christoph Burg. Unless the solo parts were taken by visiting players, these might have been the local performers who played under Mozart's own direction at the keyboard. Possibly, however, he played one of the solo violins himself.

Works of this type seem to have remained popular at Salzburg, because in November 1777 we find Leopold Mozart writing to his son: 'The Archbishop has commissioned Brunetti yesterday to write to Mysliwecek and order some concertoni', two of which were delivered in the following January. That the Mozarts certainly continued to set some store by K190 we know from their later correspondence. In a letter of 11 December 1777 addressed to his son in Mannheim, Leopold suggested that he had taken too many symphonies with him and went on: 'Could you not have performed in Mannheim your Haffner music, your concertone or one of your Lodron serenades?'

This shows how father and son regarded the purpose and character of K190. Mozart himself confirmed the interest of his concertone a few days later when, before receiving his father's letter, he wrote: 'I played through my concertone to Herr Wendling on the clavier. He remarked that it was just the thing for Paris. When I play it to Baron Bagge, he's quite beside himself.' Although we may not now share the Baron's enthusiasm unreservedly, we should still be glad to have such an enjoyable piece of music from Mozart's formative years. We can also now see clearly that this concertone, archaistic as it may seem in the context of 1774, points forward, not so much to his violin concertos of 1775 as to the imaginative treatment of the concertante style in the far greater works which were to come a few years later.

Turning to the Bassoon Concerto in B flat (K191), we may perhaps seek, as for the concertone, the name of a possible soloist in the court calendar at this time which lists Heinrich Schulz and Melchior Sandmayr. One of them may well have been in Mozart's mind as the soloist, unless he received the request from some visiting virtuoso. For chronological reasons, it is certain that this concerto was not composed for Baron Thaddäus von Dürnitz, as is sometimes stated. There is no evidence that he met Mozart or knew of him before Dürnitz went to Munich in December 1774. Only then, or a little later, could he have asked Mozart to write music for him.

Besides the curious sonata for bassoon and cello (K292/196c) and the Piano Sonata in D (K284/205b), Mozart composed three bassoon concertos (one in C and two in B flat) of which unfortunately all trace is lost. Of another, in F (K196d), only the incipit survives: this work was probably not connected with Dürnitz. Thus, of the five bassoon concertos which Mozart probably wrote, we have only the one in B flat (K191), which dates from June 1774, and was probably intended for a player in Salzburg.[1]

To what extent K191 was the product of Mozart's own unaided imagination is hard to say. The bassoon had certainly been used in concertante music by French composers, and by J. C. Bach, who also wrote two concertos for it. We have some forty bassoon concertos by Vivaldi, and others by lesser German composers such as Fasch, Felix Reiner, Müthel and G. W. Ritter. But we do not know what concertos Mozart may have heard or used as models. So when he was asked for a bassoon concerto, he may simply have relied on his feeling for the timbre and expressiveness of the instrument, and on the earlier experience of writing for it in his divertimenti. As it had then only four keys, none of which could produce a B natural, a good deal of dexterous cross-fingering was essential.

The music gives the impression that Mozart was responding to a challenge. For, taken as a whole, it is confident, assertive, and finely wrought, with skilful use of the small orchestra of strings, oboes and horns. Even when writing florid passage work for the solo instrument, Mozart remains true to its dignity and sensitivity. The construction of the first movement is simple, with two main subjects. The opening tutti is strengthened by the brief appearance of a phrase in striding octaves contrapuntally exchanged between violas and basses. Mozart's treatment of the second subject is most attractive. In the tutti he gives it to the strings alone, while in the exposition the bassoon adds its own countersubject, to produce a sensuous, gently rocking effect. But in the recapitulation Mozart devises an effective interchange, giving the bassoon's melody to the strings and *vice versa*. This passage also shows how he uses the instrument's capacity for wide leaps as part of a natural melodic sequence, and not as virtuosity for its own sake.

The second movement in F is marked, rather unusually, 'Andante

[1] Another Bassoon Concerto in B flat (K. App. 230a/C14.03) has nothing to do with Mozart, though recorded and still sometimes performed under his name. It is of a later date, and on grounds of style and melody has been plausibly ascribed to François Devienne (1759–1803).

ma adagio'. It is a dreamy arioso, with muted strings which contribute to a feeling of pathos, deepened, perhaps, for the modern listener by the faint pre-echo of 'Porgi amor' in the opening phrase. The short passage which serves as a transition to its restatement shows Mozart's imaginative skill in modulation. Imagination is not, on the whole, the hallmark of the finale where (as in the Concertone) he chose the extended minuet form instead of the bolder sonata form used in the Harpsichord Concerto in D (K175). The rhythmic patterns, with much busy triplet figuration, move rather stiffly, but Mozart uses cleverly varied phrases to soften the outlines of the conventional patterns of repetition in both solo and orchestra, and introduces some variety with an arresting episode in the tonic minor.

Mozart and the Violin

For the next eleven months, Mozart wrote no more concertos of any kind. From autumn 1774 onwards he was busy with two dramatic works, which were produced in quick succession early in 1775 – the opera *La finta giardinera* at Munich on 13 January, and the 'festa teatrale' *Il rè pastore* at Salzburg on 23 April. His other principal compositions were three masses and four other smaller pieces of church music; one serenade, one symphony and one orchestral march; half a dozen piano sonatas and one set of variations. Even allowing for theatrical demands, this was one of the least productive periods of Mozart's life. Here he seems to have paused to absorb the rich musical experience of his travels and prepare himself for the remarkable outburst of creative effort which began in the spring of 1775 and lasted just over five years.

It was not perhaps a mere coincidence that the first year was marked by an unprecedented series of five concertos, all for the violin, an instrument for which Mozart had not previously composed in this form. These concertos are, moreover, personal works in the sense that, though he may not have written them primarily for himself, he undoubtedly regarded them as a vehicle for displaying his own mastery of the instrument, a mastery which became important to him in the later 1770s. But the reputation it brought him hardly lasted beyond this decade, and after that was quickly overshadowed by his phenomenal powers as a pianist. Some account of Mozart as a violinist may, then, be appropriately given here.

Shortly after his son's birth, Leopold Mozart published his *Violin-Schule*. Since the boy was brought up, as it were, in the shadow of this famous book, it was only natural that he should have become as proficient on the violin as he was on the keyboard. Schachtner recalled that when the child was about seven he played on his (Schachtner's) violin, which he liked very much and called the 'butter violin' because of its soft, full tone. He wrote:

One or two days later I came to see him again and found him amusing himself with his own violin. He at once said: 'How's your butter violin?' and went on fiddling away at his fantasia. Finally he thought a moment and said to me: 'Herr Schachtner, your violin is tuned half a quarter-tone lower than mine, if you left it tuned as it was last time I played it.'

The boy's sense of pitch proved perfectly correct. That he was schooled in the habit of regular practice at least as early as 1770, we learn from letters exchanged later with his father, who lamented, after his son had left on his long journey in 1777, how he missed the sound of his practising. These letters also tell us something about his playing. Mozart's powers seem to have developed rapidly, for on 27 November 1770, when still under fifteen, he was appointed *Konzertmeister* in the Salzburg Court Orchestra, in which the Archbishop took pride and used to play himself. Mozart's mature skill sometimes proved useful on his travels. For instance, at the church of the Cajetan monastery in Vienna, in the summer of 1773, he played a Violin Concerto at a service because the organ was simply not good enough to play on. Again, at the Holy Cross Monastery in Augsburg, on 23 October 1777, he led the orchestra in a symphony, played a violin concerto in B flat by Wanhal and his own 'Strasbourger concerto' (in G, K216), 'which', he wrote, 'went like oil. Everyone praised my beautiful pure tone.' From Munich, a little earlier, he wrote: 'I played my last Cassation in B (K287/271H). They all opened their eyes. I played as if I was the finest fiddler in all Europe.' Indeed, Mozart's pride in his own technique was shared by his father, who was never one to give undue praise. 'You yourself', he replied, 'do not know how well you play the violin, if you will only do yourself credit and play with energy, with your whole heart and mind, yes, just as if you were the first violinist in Europe.' Later Leopold suggested that if his son went to Louvain he should play a violin concerto as the best way of making himself known there. Again, 'Mozart could play anything' was the opinion of Antonio Brunetti, who was the first violin and soloist in the Salzburg Court Orchestra and a friend of the Mozarts (though the family professed to be scandalised by his seduction of two girls in the city).

THE VIOLIN CONCERTOS OF 1775

When Mozart came to write his first full-scale concertos early in 1775, his understanding of the player's technique was matched by some experience in composing for the solo violin, for a little earlier he had included whole concerto movements in several orchestral works, the Divertimento in D (K131) and the Serenade in D (K204/213a). If, at this point, we ask what were his models for these movements and for the five concertos, we have to admit that at present our knowledge is rather limited. During the eighteenth century, violin concertos ranked second in number and popularity only to those for the keyboard. Largely Italian in origin, form and practice had coalesced from various types of music, such as the solo movements of the concerto grosso, and performance of instrumental solos at a number of points in the church service.

As Mozart had travelled a good deal in Italy, and as concertos by Italian composers were also popular north of the Alps, we might reasonably expect to be able to say which of them had influenced his concertos of 1775. Unfortunately, we really know very little about what Italian violin music he actually heard. He met Nardini at Augsburg in June 1763 and again at Florence in April 1770, when they played together. We know also that Mozart was friendly with a pupil of Nardini, the gifted English violinist Thomas Linley, and played violin music with him at Florence in April 1771. But what they played we do not know. Again, Mozart may have met Viotti at Turin in June 1770, but as the latter had written none of his concertos by then, Mozart can only have heard him (if at all) play music by other composers. It is also fairly certain that Mozart met Pugnani at Turin late in January 1771. But, in terms of definite models, all this is vague. More general, and perhaps more likely, is the possible influence of Vivaldi, whose numerous concertos remained widely popular after his death in 1741, and whose style was absorbed into the music of the next generation in which Mozart's own command of violin composition grew to maturity.

This, then, is the background to the concertos of 1775. We may wonder why he came to compose the first in B flat (K207, the autograph dated 14 April) in the strenuous days before *Il rè pastore* was staged on the 23rd in honour of the Archduke Max Franz's visit to Salzburg. Did the Archbishop first command one concerto for this festive occasion and then continue to urge Mozart to write four others? Or were all five composed specifically for Brunetti (sometimes stated, but without evidence, as a fact)? Or did Mozart himself, having supplied the first concerto, then write the others to gratify a nine-month creative urge, and to provide himself with the pleasure of future performance?

The Concerto in B flat (K207) is a work of wayward charm and prodigality of melodic invention, qualities which amply compensate for whatever it may lack in thematic elaboration and expressiveness. It is pure entertainment music, tinged with the ardour of *galanterie*; it breathes the fragrance of a spring evening in the Mirabell gardens in Salzburg. Within the rather loose sonata form of the first movement Mozart has strung together some delightful tunes in a well-contrasted sequence. Each of the melodic groups in the tutti is followed by the same striking quasi-buffo phrase which, rather unusually, Mozart does not use again at all. The solo enters with a florid version of the first subject, and then introduces the second, a smooth melody in F, which is extended at some length. The solo plunges into the development with an angular phrase in C minor which it leads through a turbulent G minor into the calmer waters of the tonic and the recapitulation. The richly varied figuration of the solo part adds much to the almost athletic momentum of the whole movement.

The Adagio, in E flat, is a graceful, murmurous affair, with attractive varieties of pace in its melodic flow, and one or two mild structural surprises. For instance, the long-drawn melody uttered by the solo at its first entry is heard only on that occasion. As this entry proceeds, Mozart recalls the first theme of the opening tutti, but totally ignores the second until he brings it back most effectively in the recapitulation. Here he first states it in brief imitation of strings and wind and then gives it to the soloist. There is certainly poetry in this movement, but it seems impersonal.

The finale, Presto, is a chattering dialogue, in a free rondo form, between solo and orchestra, cast in lightly diversified patterns of sound. The usual two groups of themes in the opening tutti are rounded off by a brisk little codetta which precedes, and immediately succeeds, the first entry of the solo. A new melody is divided, most wittily, between the soloist and the violins. In the development, while Mozart makes much play with a stepwise rising theme from the opening tutti, he is irresistibly drawn back to the little codetta, which indeed provides a piquant ending to the concerto. The style of the finale, its élan and vigour, suggests that here Mozart was touched by the spirit not of his friend and fellow court musician Michael Haydn, but of the latter's brother Joseph, some of whose music he certainly knew at this time.

On 14 June, exactly two months after K207, Mozart completed K211, the first of his three violin concertos in D. If K207 bears a distinctly Germanic stamp, its successor is unmistakably French. (This divergence is typical of the composer's youthful eclecticism.) To some extent K211 is a static work, for it marks no advance in thematic elaboration, but relies rather on a juxtaposition of contrasted ideas, and the orchestra shows even less individuality than in K207. Its accompaniment of the solo part is certainly of limpid delicacy, but here it is rather unadventurous. Again, in K211 the subjects stated in the opening tutti are used in the solo part with greater regularity than in K207.

Another feature of K211 is the divertimento-like brevity of its first movement, which comprises only 126 bars. The solo bustles along in a flurry of tightly knit triplets contrasting with passages of wide leaps and more open figuration. The construction is regular and obvious. Here and there we find some agreeable inventiveness, such as the statement of the second theme where a little up-thrust on the violas is immediately replaced by broken figures on the violins while the bass line passes to the violas – a simple but characteristically elegant touch.

The pleasant though unadventurous Andante is little more than an extended aria for violin, with a very light accompaniment, in the manner of an opéra-comique. Nor does the concluding Rondeau (the French form of the word is significant) show any marked originality. Again, the solo is continuously prominent, and in the very opening bars itself states the main theme. A short transition passage in D minor provides some variety in the shape of the solo line and in the accompaniment, but in general the movement lacks diversity, and almost every bar is pervaded by the rather artificial charms of *galanterie*.

Such, too, is the consistent character of the music that Mozart was to write in the next three months – principally the short Divertimento in F (K213), the fine, long Serenade in D (K204), two lesser symphonies and two marches. All the more surprising, then, is the sudden sublimation of the *style galant* which Mozart achieved in the third Violin Concerto of this year, K216, in G, completed on 12 September. For this is one of the masterpieces of his youth, in which he retains much of the refined, elegant idiom but blends it with a new spaciousness of construction and the sinewy strength that we associate with his later music.

What may have caused the sudden deepening of Mozart's art during this summer we do not know. This G major Concerto shows it most, perhaps, in an imaginative quality of invention which is not only reflected in the general expressiveness of the music but also gives some happy individuality to the lower strings and the wind. The broad, clearly defined themes stated in the opening tutti are impelled by a nervous energy that is maintained throughout the soloist's entry. Especially attractive is the second melody which flows off into a striking, springy phrase but is not heard again until the recapitulation. The development opens with a brief tutti in D minor preliminary to a fresh theme on the violin which moves through E minor, D minor, C major and G back to the tonic – an arresting and brilliantly effective sequence.

The Andante, in D, runs to a mere 48 bars, but contains the heart of the concerto. It stands high among all Mozart's rapturous slow movements of the dreamy type. It may be ranked with that of the Piano Concerto in C (K467), with which it has some features in common – broken triplet accompaniment, muted violins, pizzicato lower strings, and simple purity of line. Its quality is heard at its best in the development, where the modulation through B minor, E minor and ultimately A major illustrates Mozart's mastery of the art of poetic suspense.

The finale is a vivacious, cleverly diversified rondo, in which he blends fertility of invention with a whimsical delight in surprise. The main theme recurs five times, thrice contrasted with a subsidiary which is also heard in the dominant and introduces the second episode, in E minor. But the conventional rondo form and the easy lilt of 3/8 are broken by two staider episodes in ¢. The first, in G minor, has the stately air of a haunting pavane, played by the soloist, supported by piquant overlapping pizzicato phrases on the violins and the lower strings (the violas being omitted):

Ex.1

while the oboes contribute effectively to the harmony of the middle section. These twelve striking bars lead straight into the second episode, based on a simple tune in the tonic major, marked 'allegretto', and in two sections:

Ex.2

Each of them is stated first by the solo and then repeated by the wind above a flurry of triplets on the violin. (Recent research has identified this two-section tune as a Hungarian folk melody known as the 'Strasbourger'. Hence we know that it was this Concerto in G which should be identified as the 'Strasbourger Concerto' and not, as usually stated, that in D (K218).) It is such graceful variations of pace and mood, enlivened by imaginative use of the wind, that make the whole of this rondo so engaging. It ends with the recapitulation of the main theme right through to the final codetta on oboes and horns. To finish thus, rather than with a conventional climax, was a stroke of genius. In this touch of almost theatrical grace, the movement bows itself off the stage with a whimsical chuckle.

The autograph of the Concerto in D major (K218) is dated October 1775. Mozart must therefore have completed it within seven weeks, at the most, of K216. A general comparison shows both loss and gain. In K218 we find that the quality of reflectiveness and the measured interplay of solo and orchestra are replaced by a new brilliance of timbre and the more or less continuous flow of the solo part. Mozart uses the horns and oboes in a bolder, more assertive style. His fertility of melodic invention rises to a new level of exuberance. So much so, indeed, that in the first movement, although he uses normal key relationships and a generous outline of sonata form, the sheer wealth of material makes regularity almost impossible. Instead, Mozart takes delight in the unexpected, and in the unpredictable regrouping of melodies, either in their entirety or in abridgement. For instance, the theme of the opening tutti (repeated from the third aria, 'Aer tranquillo', in *Il rè pastore*) is restated by the soloist, but is not discussed at all in the development, and does not recur in the recapitulation. Here, however, at bar 146 we find seven bars of a melody from the exposition, followed at once by an abridged section of the opening tutti. This sort of ingenuity lends a keen edge to the hearer's expectancy which Mozart further heightens by some brilliant passage work, for example, at the close of the exposition where – all within barely twenty bars – the modulations ripple from B minor, through E minor, A major, G major, to E minor and back to the tonic.

Mozart cast the 'Andante cantabile', in A, in a modified type of sonata form without development, and gave the soloist almost no rest except in the opening and closing bars. Such a passage as this, in E major, with its compact echo, effects typifies the luminous quality of this very lovely movement:

Ex.3

It ends with a delicate half-statement, on a repetition of part of the opening subject, varied by a neat displacement of rhythm. Mozart repeated this opening subject again, whether consciously or not, almost note for note as the second refrain in the 6/8 section of the finale. (There are other thematic cross-references in this closely knit concerto.)

The finale, again marked 'rondeau', is remarkable for two things – the sheer speed of the musical thought, accentuated by alternating sections of 2/4 and 6/8, and the fascinating variety of the slower interludes. One is also struck by Mozart's infallible sense of proportion and timing; no episode lasts too long, and the many changes of pace are perfectly calculated. He uses the lower register of the violin most effectively, notably in the third of the sections marked 'Andante grazioso'. Here the melodies seem to have the flavour of folk tunes, and Mozart heightens this impression by a sort of drone bass produced by the oboes doubling at the octave the sustained low G of the solo:

Ex.4

Like the finales of K216 and K219, this rondeau dies away quietly. This is perhaps the place to mention the supposed extensive melodic debt of K218 to a violin concerto in the same key by Boccherini, a debt which many writers on Mozart (including Einstein) have accepted as a fact. Since, however, the work by Boccherini is now regarded as unauthentic,[1] Mozart's 'indebtedness' need no longer be taken into account.

The autograph of the Concerto in A (K219) is dated 20 December 1775, so that twelve weeks at the most separate it from K218, but it is conceived on a wholly different plane. The first movement, in particular, combines aristocratic poise with crystalline freshness and brilliant invention. The elegance conceals much strength; there is a new spaciousness of design, in which brilliant passage work is used more architecturally than before, and far less for its

[1] No MS source has been traced. The first and only edition appeared in 1924. See Yves Gérard, *Thematic, Bibliographical and Critical Catalogue of the Works of Boccherini*, London, 1969, pp. 546–8.

own sake. Mozart sustains a better balance between soloist and orchestra, and treats the latter more homogeneously, dispensing with the agreeable but rather quirky wind solos of K218.

Conventionally enough, the opening tutti, marked 'allegro aperto', states the two main subjects (the first a striding arpeggio figure) and a coda

Ex.5

all in the tonic. Then Mozart introduces the soloist, on a rising triad, to play seven bars in slow, arioso style, over murmuring violins. Only after this does he resume the allegro with a new melody for the soloist, accompanied by the striding arpeggio of the tutti. Some rapid passage work leads to a repeat of Ex. 5, the last notes of which Mozart takes up as the first phrase of another subject:

Ex.6

He uses this figure, in fact, as one of the springboards of the movement, for it introduces several sections in the development. Its last appearance is the most effective: with this rising arpeggio the movement dies away, very simply, on a sort of unanswered question.

For the rapturous Adagio Mozart chose the key of the dominant, E major, which he used so rarely but nearly always to suggest or express quiet content. (One thinks of 'Zeffiretti lusinghieri' in *Idomeneo*.) The two principal melodies, from which most of the music is constructed, are stated in the opening tutti – the first in smoothly flowing semiquavers, the second broken by the throbbing rhythm of broken demisemiquavers. The orchestra has practically no dialogue with the soloist, but supplies a rich harmonic background to the lovely cantilena. All the more effective is the little touch of canonic writing which culminates in the solo entry at the recapitulation.

The finale, another rondo marked 'tempo di minuetto', opens coolly and elegantly enough with the solo stating the main theme, followed by an important second group which ends (as in K218) on a rising arpeggio:

Ex.7

Another melodic group follows, in the dominant, and after a normal development the first episode (F sharp minor) raises the temperature a little. It is broken only by the figure marked *a* in Ex. 7; the music shifts to D major, then to B minor, and back to a cadenza on the dominant of F sharp minor – an arresting passage. A brief recurrence of the tutti leads to the truly astonishing second episode, in A minor. This consists of a sequence of five melodies of which Mozart took the first, second, fourth and fifth directly from Hungarian (or, in eighteenth-century terms, 'Turkish') folk music;

the third, based on a short chromatic figure, he seems to have composed himself in the same style. (His source for some of these tunes was possibly Michael Haydn, then recently back from a visit to Hungary.) Perhaps the most striking of all is the second, which Mozart had used three years earlier in his ballet music *Le Gelosie del Serraglio*:

Ex.8

To its jagged leaps he now added violent sforzandi and a jarring bass, so that it must have sounded quite outlandish to contemporary hearers. After this, the recurrence of the opening tutti, for the fifth time, seems a little conventional, but there is a piquant passage where Mozart sustains one of the tunes instead of shifting it to E major as at all its previous appearances. This rondo, too, ends rather quizzically on the rising arpeggio, which thus forms a thematic link with the first movement.

As a pendant to this group of Mozart's authentic concertos of 1775, there may be mentioned a work in F for violoncello (K206a) of which the autograph, once in Paris but now unfortunately lost, bore the inscription 'Concerto per il Violoncello del Sig: Cav. Amadeo Wolfgango Mozart nel Marzo 1775'. This work thus immediately preceded K207 and one wonders whether he intended it for one of the court orchestra's cellists who had perhaps played in the Concertone of 1774. Though only the first six bars are known and the work was probably never finished, it shows that Mozart was at least interested in the violoncello as a full solo instrument.

SOME SINGLE MOVEMENTS FOR VIOLIN AND ORCHESTRA

In October 1777 Leopold Mozart referred to 'an Adagio for Brunetti' which his son had written because the original was 'too studied'. It is almost certain that this Adagio is the movement in E major, K261, which is in the same key as the slow movement of K219, and of which the autograph simply bears the year '1776'. But it is difficult to see how K261 is less 'studied'. Mozart gives it a subtle difference of tone-colour by using flutes instead of oboes. By marking the violins in the orchestra 'con sordini' throughout, he heightens the intimacy with a feeling of remoteness while making the soloist more prominent. The rhythms, especially in the second subject, are springier, with a liberal flow of triplet figures. A short but striking B minor episode, which takes the place of the development, enriches the harmonic interest. These fifty-five bars are, in fact, one of the gems of Mozart's lyrical genius. What a very fortunate player Brunetti was! This Adagio was, incidentally, the first of Mozart's works to be arranged for a flute-clock: this clock is still extant in the Heyer Collection in the University of Leipzig.

Another delightful single movement is the Rondo in B flat (K269/261a). It has been accepted that this is the rondo for Brunetti which Leopold Mozart mentioned in his letter of 25 September 1777, and that it was composed in the later part of 1776 as a substitute for the finale of K207. But these are dubious assumptions. The autograph is undated, and the rondo theme (if transposed into C) is identical with the opening of one of the numbers in the ballet sketches that Mozart wrote in Paris in 1778, which suggests that the rondo came after the ballet and not before it. This, then, may not be the 'Rondo for Brunetti' assumed to have been written late in 1776, but a different work composed early in 1779 after Mozart's return from Paris. Moreover, the style – which would have ill assorted with K207 – seems not incompatible with a later date. For the music has a compact sense of unity within diversity which differentiates it from the other rondo finales of 1775. The taut, intermittent dialogue between tutti and solo, the neat interlocking between solo and first violins and the relative absence of bravura are among the features which suggest a rather more mature approach to the concerto style.

Whether or not Mozart wrote K269 for Brunetti, the latter comes into the picture yet again in the spring of 1781 when they were both in Vienna. Mozart told his father that on 8 April, in the presence of Prince Rudolf Joseph Colloredo (father of the hated Archbishop of Salzburg), Brunetti played a rondo which he (Mozart) had just composed. This was the beguiling piece in C (K373)–pure entertainment music at its best, characterised by the marking 'allegretto grazioso'. Though Mozart used the orchestra in Vienna as he had in Salzburg for his first concerto six years earlier, his more imaginative handling of it is quite clear. In the C minor episode of K373, the soloist is supported by the violins playing pizzicato over semiquaver figures on the violas, and then the oboes, in thirds, double the second violins and violas. The wind instruments are used with greater flexibility in the tuttis, and the solo part has a fresh suppleness of line with many displaced accents which add charm and a certain piquancy.

Vienna, as Mozart himself said, was 'the land of the piano'. It is therefore hardly surprising that during the last ten years of his life he completed only one more entire composition for the violin, another single movement. This he entered in his catalogue on 1 April 1785 as 'An Andante for the Violin for a Concerto', in A major, 3/4 time (K470). Unfortunately it is lost, and is known only from the first four bars which Mozart wrote out in his thematic catalogue. Einstein made the plausible suggestion that as Leopold was in Vienna this very month with his Salzburg pupil Heinrich Marchand, a fine violinist, the latter may have played K218 (the only Mozart violin concerto with a slow movement in A and in 3/4 time) in which K470 was provided as a substitute for the Andante. Finally, from about this same time, we have another glimpse of Mozart's continuing interest in violin music–the extra trumpet and drum parts which he wrote for a concerto in E minor by Viotti. Presumably he intended to add depth and brilliance to the score in a performance under his own direction, possibly with Anton Janitsch, a player from the Wallerstein household, as soloist. (This is not an isolated curiosity: Mozart wrote similar extra accompaniments for an aria in an oratorio by C. P. E. Bach.)

This little group comprises the Concertos in D (K271a/K271i), in E flat (K268/K App. C. 14.04), and the so-called 'Adélaide' Concerto. All three pose the problem of authenticity, but in very different degrees.

In the 1770s the Mozarts had the pleasant custom of celebrating on 26 July the joint 'name-day' of Anna Maria, the mother of the family, and her daughter 'Nannerl'. The celebration took the form of an evening concert, for which Mozart usually composed a new work. We know that in July 1777 the 'name-day' concert included a new violin concerto, which he played himself, and there is little doubt that this was the Concerto in D, K271a, his third in this key. For, although the autograph is lost, the copyist who made the earlier of the two extant copies transcribed faithfully the composer's own heading 'concerto per il violino di W. A. Mozart, Salisburgo, li 16 di Luglio 1777'. This date tallies perfectly with all the documentary evidence relating to the Mozart family's celebration of 1777 and to later performances of the concerto given by a Salzburg violinist named Kolb.

Somehow the autograph later passed into the possession of the famous Parisian conductor and violinist F. A Habeneck, but vanished in 1837. In 1835, however, another violinist, Eugène Sauzay, had made the above-mentioned copy for his teacher and father-in-law Pierre Baillot. Now although K271a is generally accepted as being substantially Mozart's, the music shows clear traces of alterations made perhaps by Sauzay and Baillot together to suit the Parisian taste for virtuosity. The solo part has extended passages in very high positions which are quite incompatible with the style of the 1770s. So, too, is some of the very florid ornamentation. The double-stopping, sometimes in tenths, is very much of the early nineteenth century. Some of the scoring sounds un-Mozartian, and there are some rather clumsy sequences which can hardly be authentic. But such anomalies and defects are not enough to detract from enjoyment of the concerto as a whole.

The short first movement, 'allegro maestoso', is full of thematic riches. The opening tutti states four melodies; two only of them are taken up by the solo, which adds two new ones at its first entry, two more later on and yet another in the development. Even more than in the concertos of 1775, Mozart juggles cleverly with this mass of themes throughout development and recapitulation, and keeps the hearer in continual suspense. Two other notable features of the movement are the very strong support given by oboes and horns to the strings, and the marked individuality of the divided violas. In the song-like Andante the orchestra, with strings pizzicato, supplies the melody throughout, which is rather unusual. The chief interest lies in the soaring solo line, which embellishes the theme with trills, runs and grace-notes, and is characterised by many huge leaps. The development, which begins over a dominant pedal but shifts quickly between major and minor, is a fine example of the glowing tension which Mozart could pack into little more than a dozen bars. The rondo, marked merely 'allegro', is written with an immense verve, which makes its great length (well over 500 bars) seem not excessive. There are five appearances of the principal melody, supported as in the first movement by a galaxy of other tunes, all sharply diversified and finely scored. It is notable that the two longish subjects stated by the solo at its first entry do not recur at all.

For the Concerto in E flat, K268, no complete autograph score has ever existed: it has been published from early editions which include parts for clarinets and bassoons as well as oboes and horns. There are two theories as to place and date of composition: one suggests Munich, in 1780–1, the other Vienna, in March or April 1786. Both agree in accepting the tradition, which dates from 1800, that Mozart played the work to a Munich violinist named Johann Friedrich Eck. The latter (who was also a composer, with seven published concertos to his credit) met Mozart, a friend of his family, in Munich in 1781, and also happened to be in Vienna five years later. What Mozart played from was very probably an outline score, which he then gave to Eck. At either period, Mozart's reason for not finishing the concerto would have been his preoccupation with an opera, respectively *Idomeneo* or *Figaro*. (The absence of the work from his catalogue in 1786 can be explained by the fact that Mozart entered only completed works.)

While critics generally agree that the orchestration of K268 is not Mozart's – whether it is by Eck or someone else is also uncertain – they differ strongly as to how much of the music is original. Einstein allowed that most of the first movement and the opening of the last were Mozart's, but dismissed the second as spurious. Saint-Foix believed that most of it is genuine. Blume, while accepting most of the solo and tuttis, thought that the solo included some portions transferred from the orchestra. These problems seem insoluble, and it is certainly impossible to determine how much of Mozart's original, unfinished conception is embedded in the music as we have it now. Such clear affinities as that of the opening bars of the finale with the rondo melody of the Concerto for Two Pianos are interesting, but prove little. So although this violin concerto is still occasionally recorded and performed, it hardly merits description here. But it shows that Mozart's interest in the form lasted well into his last year at Salzburg, and perhaps a good deal beyond it.

No discussion of Mozart's violin concertos would be complete without some mention of the pretty so-called 'Adélaide' Concerto, which has long been recorded and performed under Mozart's name. It was first published in 1933 by Schott, edited by Marius Casadesus from a manuscript which the preface states to be autograph, 'in private possession', but which has never been made available for inspection. The dedication of the concerto and its alleged date, July 1766, have both been highly suspect. In July 1977 Casadesus admitted that the work was a pastiche composed by himself.

Oboe and Flute Concertos

Mozart wrote these three works within about a year. Strictly speaking, there are only two concertos, because one of the two for flute, the D major (K314/285d), is his own transcription of an Oboe Concerto in C. Although the music was long published and played only in its D major form, it is the C major original, discovered in 1920 but not printed until 1948, which must be discussed here. The history of this concerto, which is also numbered K314, is interesting.

In 1775 a young oboist named Giuseppe Ferlendis left Bergamo to enter the service of the Archbishop of Salzburg. It was probably in the summer of 1777 that Mozart wrote a concerto for Ferlendis, which, though long thought lost, is now generally believed to be this work in C. During his long stay in Mannheim throughout the winter of 1777-8, Mozart met a wealthy Dutch amateur of the flute named in his letters as 'De Jean', which is probably a phonetic representation of the surname of a certain Willem Britten de Jong. 'De Jean' commissioned him to compose three quartets and three little concertos for the flute, but Mozart – as often – was dilatory.

He completed the Concerto in G (K313/285c), but then, being pressed for time, provided a second simply by transposing the oboe concerto which had been sent on to him from Salzburg. 'De Jean' seems to have been satisfied, although Mozart apparently never composed the third flute concerto.

The vivacious Oboe Concerto is distinctly French in style. Its cheerful outer movements have something of an operatic flavour, and the soloist is very much the prima donna. Written with consummate craftsmanship, the music is elegant and witty, though the relationship between solo and orchestra is still a fairly simple one. But the conception as a whole has a fluency and a perfection of timing which make it a joy to listen to. The two main subjects of the 'Allegro aperto' (a marking used in the Violin Concerto in A and the two piano concertos of 1776) are strongly contrasted – the first peremptory and compact, the second (introduced by a hesitant, sustained G on the violins) a beguiling, sprawling affair culminating in a buffo-like cadential figure:

Ex.9

which leads to the final clause in emphatic unison:

Ex.10

This is detached to play a prominent part in the development, where

Mozart introduces subtle changes in the soloist's line, and gives the answer to the second violins alone instead of to the violas and basses. Such passages are a good example of the modest dialogue between solo and orchestra. Though the tonal range of the entire movement hardly strays beyond the range of the tonic and dominant, it never sounds constrained or dull.

The mood of the slow movement, marked 'Adagio non troppo', is serene but not profound. An assertive leap of a twelfth in the second bar, which Mozart retains for each repeat of the theme, is almost the only strong interruption of the smooth melodic line, whether in solo or tutti. Perhaps the most arresting feature of the movement is the recapitulation, for here Mozart contrives a drastic and – for this period – unusual abridgement. He repeats only the first three bars of the ritornello and then introduces the soloist, but suppresses the first eight bars of his original entry.

The finale is one of the most sparkling of all Mozart's youthful rondos, alive with such dancing rhythms and brilliant variety of phrasing that here the prima donna seems transmuted into a ballerina, with the shadow of Papageno hovering prophetically in the wings. The impression of a quasi-theatrical atmosphere is strengthened by the lilt of the dominating tune uttered by the oboe in the first four bars, for it is almost identical with 'Welche Wonne, welche Lust' which Mozart put into the lips of Blonde in *Die Entführung* five years later. This rondo is very tightly knit, with few episodes to break the thread. Indeed, as a contrast to the soloist's bravura excursions, Mozart devises such a passage as this:

Ex.11

where he treats the theme in octave canon, here bringing in the solo line which he had omitted in the exposition. And how delightful is the unexpected use of the figure marked *a* on the oboe solo to lead into the penultimate return of the main theme of this rondo!

Not surprisingly, the concerto remained something of a favourite. The famous oboist Ramm played it regularly in Mannheim, and the composer himself revived it in Vienna in 1783. It is not perhaps strictly accurate to say that the D major Flute Concerto is a 'transposition' of this work for oboe. It is, rather, a reworking, with a good many differences in phrase endings and dynamics, with some changes in the melodic line and an occasional enrichment of harmony; the marking of the slow movement is altered from 'Adagio' to 'Andante'. Even without other evidence, its origin is shown by the fact that the high register of the flute is scarcely used at all.

The G major Flute Concerto (K313) has a rather puzzling background. On 10 December 1777 Mozart told his father that 'De Jean' would pay him 200 florins for composing 'three little, easy short concertos'. Three months later, he wrote again referring to 'De Jean's' commission:

Here I do not have one hour of peace. I can only compose at night, and so cannot get up early. Besides, one is not disposed to work at all times. I could certainly scribble the whole day, but a piece of music goes out into the world, and, after all, I don't want to feel ashamed for my name to be on it. And, as you know, I am quite inhibited when I have to compose for an instrument which I cannot endure.

This seems to illustrate the remarkable detachment which enabled Mozart to isolate himself from his feelings and write fine music in spite of them. Moreover, the fact that K313 is neither 'short' nor 'easy' suggests that the creative effort took possession of him and led him to produce a concerto which, in dimensions and quality, far exceeded what 'De Jean' wanted.

Though Mozart scored the concerto for the same orchestra (oboes, horns and strings) as he used in Salzburg, the texture is richer and more sonorous. While exploiting the agility of the flute to the full, he never let it run riot, and achieved a finer balance between solo and orchestra. He wrote more adventurous and varied melodies, and endowed even the linking passages with a stronger character. His range of tonal imagination now seems to be increasing.

The very marking of the first movement, 'Allegro maestoso' (which Mozart chose infrequently at this time), is significant – a connotation of dignity and power. The usual two main themes are stated in the tutti, which ends with an emphatic eight-bar ritornello. This, in whole or part, is of some structural significance. Mozart uses two bars from it to curtail the first solo entry, establishing E minor for a new melody, curiously hesitant in tone, which modulates to the dominant. After the flute has restated the second subject, it is again interrupted by part of the ritornello, here slightly modified, but quickly resumes its thread with some brilliant passage-work, including a sequence of tenths. An expanded repetition of the orchestral opening leads to this remarkable new melody on the flute, preceded by an important introductory figure *a* in the orchestra:

This D minor statement is cut short by another emphatic incursion of the ritornello, after which it is repeated in E minor. Figure *a* in Ex. 12 plays an important part in the taut, boldly modulating development, in which the flute displays its most athletic leaps, up to a double octave. From this outline, various subsidiary themes have been omitted. Mozart's exuberant melodic invention reminds one of the B flat Violin Concerto, with the difference that in three years he has learned the skill of tighter, well-integrated construction.

To say that the 'Adagio ma non troppo' is a compact essay in modified sonata form with a short central episode is merely to outline the bare bones of the movement: it does not convey its singular beauty. Mozart directs the violins and violas to play muted throughout, and sometimes, with the basses, pizzicato. This, combined with the substitution of flutes for oboes (though of rather uncertain authority), suffuses the orchestral colouring with a touch of poetry and remoteness. The opening is unusual. Horns and strings in unison announce a rising arpeggio on the dominant, which seems to establish a mood of questioning. But as the long, sinuous outlines of the first subject rise and fall, with clever changes of pace, the music gains confidence by the time the second subject is reached. Here Mozart has achieved a delicate but firm partnership between solo and orchestra which is enhanced by a later episode in B minor. The final word in quiet reaffirmation is left to the flute, which restates the first three bars of the main subject with small, effective changes in the string accompaniment. In expressive power, this movement marks a point even higher than that which Mozart reached in the Adagio of his Violin Concerto in G major.

While the marking of the finale, 'Rondo. Tempo di menuetto', is familiar, the style has matured. Virtuosity there certainly is, but as part of a balanced and beautifully calculated whole. The easy, graceful style conceals a wealth of imaginative detail and clever formal planning. Just as Mozart's varied decoration of the solo line is an endless delight, so, too, his subtle lengthening of phrases at their repeat adds the charm of the unexpected. Typical of the fine musical architecture of this rondo is the romantic E minor episode and the passage from the preceding tutti leading to it. After repeating the pretty little descending scales, Mozart gives them a fresh twist by inverting them just before the flute enters. Its new melody passes quickly to the oboes, with full orchestral support, and the flute answers with limpid scale passages:

Ex.13

–as delightful an example of concerto style as one could wish for. Tonally, the rondo is rather less bold than the first movement; indeed, after the cadenza, Mozart might seem lacking in resource when he clings remorselessly to the tonic for nearly all that was previously heard in the dominant. But he still has a formal surprise up his sleeve. Just when the movement seems to be ending, pleasantly but rather unadventurously, with the fourth return of the opening tutti, he breaks it off half-way through with twenty bars of a new, arresting solo episode, and so invigorates the conclusion of a memorable concerto. This is the sort of composition which Leopold had in mind when he wrote to his son a little earlier:

> What is slight can still be great, if it is written in a natural, flowing and easy style – and at the same time bears the marks of sound composition. . . . Good composition, sound construction – *il filo*, these distinguish the master from the bungler.

Mozart's final work for flute and orchestra is the Andante in C (K315/285e), of which the autograph – unlike that of K313 – is extant. But as it bears neither date nor place, and as the superscription is not in the composer's hand, the origin of the piece must be conjectural. Mozart probably wrote it either late in his stay in Mannheim or soon after reaching Paris, that is, in the winter of 1777 or early spring of 1778. (To assert, as Einstein does, that Mozart wrote the Andante, at 'De Jean's' request, as an alternative to the Adagio of K313, is quite unwarrantable.) The movement hinges on an arresting introductory five-chord phrase, in which the strings play pizzicato (in spreading tenths, twelfths and octaves on violins and violas) beneath the wind – a quite exceptional style of opening. The principal subject is one of the most haunting Mozart ever wrote for the flute; inevitably it brings *Die Zauberflöte* to mind, for its opening, in line and level, sounds prophetic of Tamino's first trial of his instrument. On this theme Mozart weaves the undulating patterns of the arioso, articulated by five varied returns of the opening chordal phrase, two of them on the strings alone. The most important of them occurs in the central episode, where the flute rises to a sustained D, and under it the plangent chords shift mournfully to G minor, the key which dominates the hovering transition passage leading to the recapitulation.

From this same winter, we have an interesting instance of Mozart's willingness to help a musical friend. In November 1777, he supplied extra wind parts for a flute concerto by one of his Mannheim hosts, the composer J. B. Wendling. This is an interesting parallel to Mozart's contribution to the Viotti violin concerto already mentioned.

As a pendant to the group of oboe and flute concertos, it is worth mentioning that Mozart's interest in oboe and orchestra revived in February 1783, when he began another concerto (K293/416f, in F major), at the request of Anton Mayer, the oboist of Prince Esterházy's orchestra, then in Vienna. It is sad that unknown circumstances prevented Mozart from finishing the work, for the fragment of seventy bars, fully scored only up to bar 48, suggests that it would have been a splendid piece.

The Sinfonie Concertanti

When Mozart reached Paris from Mannheim on 23 March 1778, he had virtually a new world to conquer, because most Parisian music-lovers, as distinct from the professionals, had forgotten him during the twelve years that had passed since he came among them as a child prodigy. Moreover, though times and musical taste had changed, patronage was still as essential as before, and proved hard to win. So Mozart had to spend much time scurrying to and from the houses of the nobility to give lessons. Lacking his father's guidance, he found some compensation in the advice of their old friend Baron Friedrich Melchior von Grimm. It was probably through his recommendation that Mozart received several important commissions within little over a week of arrival. One was from Jean Le Gros, the director of the *Concerts spirituels*, for a sinfonia concertante for four wind instruments, while another came from the 'Duc de Guines' (as Mozart styles him) for a concerto for flute and harp.

The sinfonia concertante was one of the most interesting musical forms which evolved during the transitional period of the mid-eighteenth century. These concertanti were an offshoot of the Italian concerto grosso and were first heard in the early 1750s. Having gradually become popular in the next ten years or so, they flourished for half a century, from about 1770 onwards, and were composed in large numbers. Though they were a hybrid form, they proved vigorous enough to coexist with the classical symphony and the concerto at their peak. One reason for this was that the latter part of the century saw the rise of the virtuoso wind players all over western Europe, and the musical public never tired of their skill. Virtuosity stimulated the growth of the concertante form. The number of solo instruments ranged from two to nine, and the variety of the possible combinations was far greater than that of the soloists in the concerto grosso. When both string and wind instruments were used, the latter generally predominated.

Melodic abundance was an outstanding characteristic. The group of solo instruments tended to state and develop its own material rather than elaborate the melodies of the opening tutti. While the sinfonia concertante flourished in many European cities, it was especially cultivated in Paris and Mannheim, where wind instruments and their players were almost deified. Considering Mozart's love of woodwind and brass, it might seem surprising that he found no opportunity to compose a sinfonia concertante during his stay of four and a half months in Mannheim. But the need to pay for his livelihood kept him very busy teaching and composing to order; moreover, he suffered some distraction through his love-affair with Aloysia Weber. In any case, the opportunity came soon enough after he reached Paris on 23 March.

Mozart's own letters describe the circumstances in which he wrote the Sinfonia Concertante in E flat (K297B) for Le Gros. On 5 April 1778 the composer told his father: 'I am now going to compose a sinfonia concertante for flute, Wendling; oboe, Ramm; horn, Punto; bassoon, Ritter.' (He had been friendly with Wendling and Ramm in Mannheim; they were among the finest players of their day and had travelled on to Paris just before Mozart. Punto, a Bohemian, was one of the great masters of the horn.) On 1 May he wrote:

There appears to be a hitch with regard to the sinfonia concertante, and I think that something is going on behind the scenes. . . . I had to write the sinfonia in a great hurry and I worked very hard at it. The four performers were and still are quite in love with it. Le Gros kept it for four days to have it copied, but I always found it lying in the same place.

Le Gros, in fact, failed to have the work performed during Mozart's stay (though it was probably played in Paris in the summer of 1779). In July Mozart said he intended to send the sinfonia back to Salzburg with some other recent compositions. But it is difficult to see what he meant by this unless he expected to recover the score, or at least a set of parts, from Le Gros. This idea seems to be contradicted by what he wrote from Strasbourg on 3 October:

Le Gros purchased from me the two overtures and the sinfonia concertante. He thinks that he alone has them, but he is wrong, for they are still fresh in my mind, and as soon as I get home I shall write them down again.

Obviously, Mozart set considerable store by this work; it is all the more unfortunate that it does not survive. For though a Sinfonia Concertante in E flat (K App. C. 14.01) is to be found in print and on gramophone records under Mozart's name, and is still performed in concerts as his, its authenticity is now seriously doubted by most scholars. For the only source is a manuscript of unknown provenance, written during the 1850s or 1860s, and the solo instruments are not those for which Mozart composed with his friends in mind. In this manuscript, oboe and clarinet replace flute and oboe. It has been suggested that the manuscript derives from a lost arrangement made by Mozart himself (at some unknown time and place), but this is hardly relevant. For the music as a whole is simply unworthy of him, although it is pleasant enough, and the first two movements – the third is distinctly banal – contain a few good passages. One has only to look at the splendid concertante-style Andante (flutes, oboes, horns, and bassoons) of the Serenade in D (K320) to see how different Mozart's genuine wind-writing is.

We can now turn to the first extant work of Mozart's in concertante form, the Concerto for Flute and Harp in C (K299). It seems that he must have been working on this concerto while he was composing the lost concertante for Le Gros. For on 31 July he wrote: 'He [the 'Duc de Guines'] has already had, for the last four months, a concerto of mine for flute and harp for which he has not yet paid me.' This nobleman (Adrien-Louis Bonnière de Souastre, Comte de Guines, to give him his full and correct style) was himself a good flautist, and his daughter a fine harp player with a memorised repertoire of 200 pieces. She also took lessons in composition from Mozart, but proved, as he recounts amusingly, a ludicrously inept pupil. Though Mozart ultimately came to despise this aristocratic family, because of their meanness to him, posterity should feel some gratitude to the Duke and his daughter whose collective talents elicited such a delightful piece of music.

As a domestic and concert instrument, the harp rose to popularity at roughly the same time as the sinfonia concertante itself. How much harp music Mozart had heard before 1778, and where, we do not know. But we do know that some twelve years later he expressed his dislike for the harp, coupling it with the flute. It is ironical that so soon after executing 'De Jean's' commission he should have received another request for flute music, this time in conjunction with the only other orchestral instrument which he found un-attractive. Yet it is surely clear that Mozart's dislike was an intel-lectual one, which he did not allow to affect his musicianship. Otherwise he could not have created such beautiful music now, for flute and harp, and later yet again for the flute alone in *Die Zauber-flöte*, where surely he must finally have exorcised his antipathy.

Although the autograph does not bear a description, this work for flute and harp is a true concertante symphony, not only in the treatment of the two solo instruments but also because of their free association, in parts of the finale, with the oboes and horns. This is an underrated work, for though it plumbs no depths it is by no means superficial. It is alive with delicate poetic feeling, and shows with what masterly resource Mozart could meet the challenge of an exceptional combination of instruments. Much of the texture is limpid and shimmering: he pours out a stream of marvellous melodies, strung like glistening pearls on the thread of his invention. He gives to the flute and the harp more themes for them to treat as entirely or largely their own than he does to the orchestral tutti.

The first movement (Allegro) is basically in sonata form with a long exposition and recapitulation, but a short development. It glows with the ardour of *galanterie*. The orchestra, with the pene-trating support of the soloists, opens with an assertive unison on the broken common chord. There quickly follows another subject uncommonly variegated in shape (see Ex. 14, opposite) and played over a discreet pizzicato in the lower strings, after which comes the usual codetta. The soloists repeat the chordal theme, and then the semibreves of Ex. 14, followed by broken scale-passages. Next, the flute states three more melodies in quick succession, with the harp in a supporting role. This whole passage is in the dominant. But a more adventurous harmonic structure leads to two more new themes, of which the second (Ex. 15, on page 47) is the only one in the entire movement fully treated by both soloists. Mozart develops it in twenty bars of shimmering light and shade, which pass through D minor, F major, C minor, C major, and lead to the recapitulation. Here he curtails the melodic abundance of the soloists, but varies the music with some pretty inversions and changes of figuration. The movement ends not with the codetta (as in several of the violin concertos), but the broken chord opening, briskly restated in canon

Ex.14

by wind and strings.

In this Allegro, Mozart occasionally divides both the violas and the cellos and basses. In the Andantino, he discards the wind and divides the violas throughout; they lie at the heart of some singularly lovely string-writing. The mood is dreamy and poetic, and the structure straightforward. There is more true dialogue for both the soloists, and the harp has a greater variety of accompaniment figures. As an example of Mozart's feeling for texture and spacing, Ex. 16, on page 49, shows a few bars after the cadenza, repeated, with the addition of the solo parts, from the opening tuttis.

In the scintillating, limpid rondo Mozart's inventiveness surges on in a tumbling spate of melody, in which five of the themes – or groups of themes – are played exclusively or largely by the soloists. But they do not have the stage entirely to themselves. In half a dozen passages oboes and horns, singly or together, stand out from the orchestra as concertante instruments. They are prominent at the very opening, where they restate the gavotte-like first theme, and later they share several splendid episodes with the flute and the harp. Mozart treats the harp more generously than he did in the first movement. For instance, it alone announces the new subject which enters at the end of the first tutti. In another striking passage, the harp provides a rippling accompaniment to the oboes under the sustained high C of the flute. It is this same theme, played again by the oboes fortified by the horns, which brings the rondo to a powerful close. In this concerto, even more than in the finales of the violin concertos, Mozart beguiles the hearer with the unexpected – new groupings and regroupings of the themes, and many delightfully varied decorations of the melodic lines. The whole work is alive with a sense of liberation and optimism. How sadly was this to be changed and frustrated by the later events of 1778 – the death of the composer's mother, his own deepening sense of failure, and his slow, dejected return from Paris to the suffocating provincialism of Salzburg!

Mozart's interest in the concertante style by no means ended with his departure from Paris. He lingered again in Mannheim to sample its musical delights, and in mid-November began to compose a Concerto for Violin and Piano in D (K315f), which he intended for the Académie des Amateurs with the leader, Ignaz Fränzl, and himself as soloists. But the death of the Elector seems to have caused the Académie to disband; deprived of incentive, Mozart broke off composition at the 120th bar, having scored it fully up to bar 74. The majestic opening suggests that this would have been a fine work[1].

Mozart reached Salzburg on 15 January 1779, and to his intense chagrin was reinstated in the Archbishop's service as court and cathedral organist. As his spirits flagged, so did his creative urge. For in the next seven months or so he produced only about a dozen compositions, including the Concerto for Two Pianos, the Mass in C, two small-scale symphonies and the brilliant but straggling 'Posthorn' Serenade – mostly works of the fairly familiar Salzburg type. Then, in the late summer or autumn – if the chronology is correct – the concertante style blazed up for the last time and produced one of the great masterpieces of this or any other period in Mozart's life – the Sinfonia Concertante in E flat for Violin and Viola (K364).

The doubt about chronology is unavoidable, because no autograph source survives, except for one leaf of a draft for the first

[1] The movement has been completed for performance by Robert D. Levin (material on hire from Bärenreiter).

46

Ex.15

movement and some cadenzas. We can only guess who were the soloists on whom Mozart lavished music of such exceptional virtuosity. They may have been those for whom, with an unknown 'cellist, he intended his Triple Concerto in A (K320e), of about the same date. This, like the Concerto for Piano and Violin, remained a magnificent torso. (On the basis of its 134 bars, 51 of them fully scored, Otto Bach completed the movement and had it published by Spina in 1871.) The absence of clarinets from K364 and K320e suggests that both these concertantes were composed for performance in Salzburg rather than in Mannheim, though it is not impossible that some virtuosi soloists from the latter city (including perhaps Fränzl) visited Mozart after his return home.

Compared with the other music Mozart wrote in the spring and summer of 1779, K364 is a giant. It towers up as would the Matterhorn if transplanted to stand among the gentle foothills and lesser peaks that rise from the Salzburg plain. Gone are the last traces of the galanterie of the earlier 1770s and the playful charm of such a work as the symphony in B flat composed in July 1779. In their place appear a new mood and a new depth of sonority. Listening to K364, it is hard to believe that the orchestra is the same as the one used for the violin concertos of 1775. The increased richness of sound is due partly to the fact that there are many passages where most of the instruments play *divisi*, and partly to the regular support given by the soloists to the tuttis. The texture gains in brightness from the solo viola part being notated in D, so that this instrument is tuned up a semitone and consequently stands out from the violas of the orchestra.

As already mentioned in connection with the Flute Concerto in G, Mozart used the marking 'maestoso' infrequently, and always with a purpose. Rarely did he use it with such significance as he did for the first movement of K364. (Indeed, it colours the whole work.) In many passages, it seems to carry something of the connotation of Elgar's 'nobilmente'. For this Concertante is a proud, deeply expressive masterpiece, in which the sombre glow of passion so broods over the waters of Mozart's creative imagination that gleams of exultation flicker in alternation with the shadows of despair. Yet here, as in the great works of his Viennese period, Mozart does not allow deep feeling to disturb the unity or balance, and reconciles perfectly the demands of the soloists with the organic conception of the work as a whole. Time and again, with masterly control, he

builds up climaxes to a point of almost unbearable tension and then resolves it without any sense of bathos.

In the opening tutti of the first movement Mozart announces six themes and then, true to the spirit of the concertante style, lavishes as many more new melodies, mostly stated by the soloists, on the exposition and on the central section which is hardly a true development. Throughout this long tutti the music hardly leaves the tonic, and its character is emphasised by the rhythm of the opening phrase:

Ex.17

which is typical of the Mannheim composers from whom Mozart learned so much. (Karl Stamitz, for example, began one of his symphonies with the identical phrase, and Mozart himself repeated it, with some slight changes, in various later works, such as the Wind Octet K375 and the Piano Concerto K482, both in E flat.) Throughout this Allegro this cardinal phrase recurs, sometimes abridged, to mark a climax, a pause or change of direction. After the introductory statement, a vigorous rising figure on cellos and basses leads to a fresh melody played alternately by horns and oboes over pizzicato strings. This is immediately followed by a long, thrilling crescendo of a type which Mozart must surely have heard at Mannheim. Here he builds it up in two phrases: the first rises, on the violins, chromatically in expanding groups through an octave and a half; the second, in shorter phrases on the lower strings, rumbles beneath syncopated figures on the violins and the antiphonal calls of horns and oboes on a modification of Ex. 17. As the tumult dies away, with gently dropping phrases on the oboes, the soloists enter in sustained octave unison – Ex. 18, opposite – a moment of pure enchantment. The soloists discuss a new, flowing melody, punctuated by a further modification of Ex. 17, after which another new theme, in C minor, enters on the violin. A long dialogue between the soloists leads to an open, leaping theme in the dominant which they expand in statement and answer before uniting boldly in thirds to promulgate yet another melodic group.

A brilliant tutti follows, punctuated by the modified rhythm of Ex. 17 on the winds. A brief recurrence of the 'Mannheim' crescendo reintroduces the soloists with a new theme in C minor,

Ex.18

modulating to G minor. Some more brilliant passage work, under the lovely echoing interplay of the winds, leads to the recapitulation, where some surprising things happen. After but six bars it breaks off; the soloists enter on their octave unison and add three short new melodies in quick succession. Then one of the themes suppressed in the shortened tutti reappears on the wind with entirely new interjections from the soloists. Three times in this absorbing recapitulation their roles are reversed, with the viola playing what had originally been given to the violin. Now, as in the slow movement, the fine cadenza is Mozart's own. Far from being a display of virtuosity, it heightens the tension, and shows that he already has the same mastery of two-part string writing that he showed four years later in the Violin and Viola Duets K423–4. In the short closing tutti we hear the final mutterings of the 'Mannheim' crescendo on the lower strings just before the brusque coda.

For intensity matched by mastery of construction, the C minor Adagio bears comparison with any of the finest slow movements in Mozart's later concertos. Deeply eloquent as the music is, it seems to be not so much a complaint as an expression of weariness and despair, suggested by the semiquaver phrases which throb persistently on the violas throughout the opening tutti. What the solo violin plays in its eight-bar entry is really a variation on the melody of that tutti, and the viola's answer varies and embellishes the pattern to an even higher degree. The whole episode, including the extension which leads to the second subject, is a wonderful example of Mozart's skill in diversifying figuration with subtle, finely controlled changes of pace. The second subject is played by the strings alone, still in E flat (Ex. 19, opposite). The movement of the parts has the simple tranquillity of a slow movement in one of the great string quintets. The soloists decorate this melody in canonic imitation which leads into a short tutti. In the development and recapitulation Mozart sustains the tension by his unpredictable treatment of the solo lines: sometimes he thins out the texture within the symmetry of statement and answer, sometimes he draws it together. The power of the passages where the soloists close ranks, so to speak, is marvellously contrasted with the lyrical flow of their spacing out, as in the section of the recapitulation shown in Ex. 20. The sixteen-bar cadenza ends in a chromatic climax of almost unbearable poignancy.

The finale, marked 'presto', is a rondo with two episodes: the

themes are sharply defined, and the form is easy to follow. As if in relief from the tensions of the Andante, the music moves at a tremendous pace and seems to exult in a freedom which is still the freedom of youth but tempered now by a mature sense of proportion within a clearly defined organic whole. While less prodigal of invention than, for instance, in the finale of the flute and harp concerto, Mozart remains true to the concertante principle, and gives the soloists several melodies which they keep almost entirely to themselves. Throughout the movement the wind, which played a subsidiary role in the Andante, comes to life again, especially in the cheerful tune bandied about between oboes and horns near the end of the exposition and often heard later. As in the first movement, though less frequently, Mozart used the telling inversion of the soloists, giving to the viola the restatement of themes originally heard on the violin and *vice versa*.

At the start, the effervescent bustle of the music offsets the rather square eight-bar symmetry of the opening statement and answer. But as new ideas begin to flow in, phrases become longer and rhythms more flexible. Except for part of the first episode (which is in the dominant) and a few short later passages of transient modulations, the tonality of most of the movement remains firmly rooted in the tonic. Consequently, any strong shift of key becomes all the more effective, as occurs, for instance, early in the second episode. A short tutti ends in C minor, and is followed, after a bar's pause, by three brusque chords which shift the harmony to G major. Then the viola plunges into an unprepared A flat, and takes wing on the melody of the solo's original first entry, unheard for so long.

Another continual joy is the way Mozart alters the line of his themes:

Ex.21

This simple tune from the opening tutti is reshaped at a later repeat on the viola, answered at once by this angular outline on the violin:

Ex.22

Within this kaleidoscopic framework, Mozart allows himself little opportunity for the expansive build-up of exciting climaxes such as pervaded the first movement. But in a passage like this:

Ex.23

he shows how simply he contrives to fuse the soloists into a brief flash of tension. The movement ends brilliantly with some dazzling scale-passages, which take the soloists up to the highest possible register, leading to an admirably concise coda. This great double concerto (for such it really is) surely marks a climacteric in Mozart's life. Whatever emotional content we may now read into the music, the sustained richness of form, harmony and sonority offers unmistakable evidence of a new surge of imaginative power. We can also detect in this forward-looking masterpiece a sense of resolution and a concentrated seriousness of expression which point even beyond the splendours of *Idomeneo* to the full flowering of Mozart's genius in Vienna.

The Horn Concertos

Mozart wrote all his works for solo horn and orchestra in the 1780s. At this time the instrument still lacked valves and its diatonic range was far more limited than that of the modern horn. This was because the player, using lip pressure alone, could produce only fifteen open notes of the harmonic series, four of which were not in perfect tune. But by gradually moving his hand deeper into the bell, the player could lower the pitch and produce a number of stopped notes, which would bring the four out-of-tune notes into tune. By the same means he could also fill in the smaller gaps in the upper part of the series. Since, however, even on a modern valved instrument Mozart's concertos are a very hard test of skill, we can appreciate the very formidable challenge they offered to the player of his own day, who had to acquire delicate, perfectly timed co-ordination of lip and hand. Only a very few could meet this challenge adequately. The supreme virtuoso was, by common consent, the Bohemian Punto, whom Mozart had met in Paris. Not far behind him in excellence were three or four others, including a French player, J. J. Rodolphe, Spandau, probably of Brandenburg, and the Austrian Leutgeb, for whom Mozart composed all his horn concertos.

Joseph (not Ignaz, as he is often called) Leutgeb had entered the Salzburg court orchestra as a horn-player in the earlier 1760s, and later was also listed among its violinists. He became a friend of the Mozart family at least as early as 1763 and developed a close relationship with the composer which lasted until the latter's death. This was the longest of all Mozart's musical friendships. Leutgeb also enjoyed some reputation as a composer of concertos for his instrument. He seems to have won fame quickly as a soloist, for he visited Vienna in 1767, Paris in 1770, and Milan in 1773. In Paris he won high praise for the singing quality of his tone and his phenomenal accuracy. In 1777 he left Salzburg, and settled in Vienna where his wife had inherited a cheesemonger's business. He died, in quite prosperous circumstances, in 1811.

One characteristic of all solo music composed for the hand horn was directly due to the acoustic limitations of the harmonic series, which ordained that nine of its sixteen notes should lie close together in the highest of the three octaves. Consequently, most of the melodic line of any solo part lay within this octave and a few notes below it. This high, relatively limited register gave horn music its penetrating, powerful quality. Composers accepted this limitation and adapted their invention accordingly. One excellent composer was Franz Anton Rössler (or Rosetti), *Capellmeister* to Prince Öttingen-Wallerstein. Rössler wrote a dozen or more concertos, some of which may have influenced Mozart. Attractive as many of their melodies are, they cannot compare with the poetic subtlety of Mozart's invention. Moreover, the latter enjoyed the continued stimulus provided by Leutgeb's exceptional gifts. It seems clear, however, that he deliberately did not overtax them in terms of duration. For the first and last movements of the concertos average well under 200 bars in length; this is much shorter than the same movements of most of the other concertos, and suggests that Mozart realised there was a physical limit even to Leutgeb's powers.

Since all the horn concertos date from the time of Mozart's maturity, we might expect them to be free from historical uncertainty and textual imperfections. But this is not so. Three of the five which he wrote (or intended to write), namely K417, K447, K495, are complete in three movements, more or less as he left them, but the date of K447 is conjectural, indeed disputed. Another concerto is in two movements only (K412 and K514), is of uncertain date, and poses an acute problem of authenticity. The earliest of all, K371, is dated precisely but consists only of the final rondo, with some fragments of a first movement. In his dealings with Leutgeb, as with other soloists in Vienna, Mozart was clearly on occasion pressed for time.

We know nothing about any contemporary performance of any of Mozart's horn concertos except possibly the Rondo in D, K371. He dated its autograph 21 March 1781, only twelve days after he arrived in Vienna, and three days after he had alluded to Leutgeb in a letter to his father. In other letters of late March and early April, Mozart mentions some concerts he was giving under the patronage of Prince Rudolf Joseph Colloredo, and it seems a fair assumption that this Rondo for horn was written for one of them, possibly that held on 8 April, at which the Rondo in C (K373) for violin and orchestra was performed. Mozart composed the whole of the solo part and scored the first sixty bars almost completely. Though the rest is only partly scored, the piece has been completed for performance without much difficulty (by Waldemar Spiess, published by Breitkopf). It is wholly delightful, engaging and straightforward, and notable for its jaunty main theme which is quite unlike any of Mozart's quicker horn melodies. To accompany a subsidiary tune he introduces, on the violins, an undulating figure which is virtually the same as the melody that dominates the orchestra throughout Act II scene 9 of *Figaro*. In this Rondo Mozart begins to show how eloquently he responded to Leutgeb's ability to sustain a singing tone with great accuracy – a quality which the Parisian critics had noted in 1770.

Mozart composed another concerto in D for Leutgeb (K412/ 386b), probably towards the end of 1782, in two movements only, an Allegro and a Rondo. In the original autograph, the former is complete and fully scored for strings, oboes and bassoons, but the latter is a draft score for strings only. This is of great interest because in between and above the staves Mozart wrote, in colloquial, sometimes coarse Italian, a stream of warning, exhortation and abuse addressed in banter to Leutgeb. It is as if Mozart had his friend sitting beside him while he composed, and were imagining his response to the challenge of performance. In translation these unique phrases run thus:

At the close of the ritornello: 'To you, Mr Donkey' – in the applause at the theme: 'Come on – quick – get on with it – like a good fellow – courage – and get it over now' (at the conclusion). And again: 'You ass – oh what a horrid noise – who? – oh dear (at a repeatedly recurring F sharp) – well done, poor chap! What a ballsup! (when the subject recurs) – how you make me laugh! – help! (at a repeated E flat) – have a breather! (at a pause) – go on, go on – that's going a bit better (when the theme returns) – haven't you really finished? – you dreadful swine! How charming you are! Dear little man! little donkey! aha – take a breath! But do play at least one note, old cock! (at a repeated C sharp) – jolly good! – you're going to bore me for the fourth time, and thank God it's the last (at the fourth repetition of the theme) – Oh finish, please! Curse you – bravura as well? (at a short run). Good – a sheep could trill like that (at a shake) – you've done? Thank heaven – enough, enough!'

(From these remarks, taken with the dedication of K417 and some anecdotes about Leutgeb, which are of much later origin, it has generally been assumed that he really was a simpleton. But his successful career rather seems at variance with this; perhaps Mozart only saw one side of his character.)

Musically, this Rondo presents a problem. For it has always been printed in a text derived not from the autograph of 1782 but from what has been accepted as a more complete 'version' finished by the composer on 6 April 1787 (later numbered K514), which was not, however, entered in his own catalogue. The reason for this 'omission' is now clear, because it has recently been discovered that this 'version', which is for strings and oboes, without bassoons, is not in Mozart's hand at all, but in that of an unknown copyist! Though the melodic line is pretty well the same, the orchestration differs substantially from that of the 1782 draft score, and cannot be regarded as authentic. But as that autograph vanished in the last war and was unpublished, the 'version' of 1787 is the only text available.

Both movements of K412 are very short: the first has 143 bars, the second 140. Simple – almost artless – in form, they serve as entertainment music and to display the soloist's virtuosity. They are largely devoid of the poetry of the later concertos. For the most part, the strings generate a gentle current of sound, dappled by the intermittent ripples of the woodwind (more effective, naturally, in the first than in the second movement), above which the horn floats serenely. Mozart tested Leutgeb's technique quite severely in the first movement with some passages of brisk semiquavers. As in some of the violin concertos, there is great play in transitions with a codetta, a tight, angular figure, from the end of the first subject. The second, in the dominant, is the more interesting and supple. As an appendage to it, Mozart gives the solo a sequence of wide leaps in minims, presumably in respite from the testing semiquavers. It seems unlikely that Mozart did not compose a middle movement, but no trace of it survives. The rondo is straightforward, in the lilting 6/8 time which he used for all these finales. There is a strong family resemblance here; to eighteenth-century audiences, familiar with the sound of the hunting horn, the melodic type of the opening refrain must have proved very attractive. Four statements of it are punctuated by four subsidiary themes. The second entry of the refrain is in bold four-part canon, leading to a D minor melody of which the last section, in F major, provides an unmistakable instance of Mozart's gift for parody. Here, in the solo line (Ex. 24, p. 61), he adapts almost note for note part of the Gregorian melody in the famous *Lamentationes Jeremiae Prophetae*, to which the names of Hebrew letters were sung, and so on for another five bars. The parody accounts for the rather stiff, repetitive melodic line. Since this chant was a familar part of the Easter service, Mozart's audience could hardly have missed the point of the musical joke.

He inscribed the autograph of the next concerto (K417, in E

flat) in German, thus: 'Wolfgang Amadeus Mozart took pity on Leutgeb, donkey, ox and simpleton, at Vienna 27 May 1783'. This was the period when the second and third of the string quartets dedicated to Haydn were germinating in Mozart's mind, and when he was still working on the great Mass in C minor. Barely three weeks after he inscribed K417 to Leutgeb, Constanze gave birth to their first child, a boy who lived less than five weeks. Such is the background to this genial concerto, in which the mood of good humour is seldom darkened by minor tonalities.

This is the first horn concerto of which all three movements survive, although the autograph of the second movement is lost, and that of the third is defective at the end. Fortunately, the first edition of 1802 fills the gap. The strings are supported by oboes and horns, both confined almost entirely to the tuttis. The first movement is the only one in all these concertos marked 'maestoso', an adjective which, as we have seen, had a definite connotation for Mozart. For here he composes on a more generous plan than in K412, and with a sense of dignity which we met in such similarly marked works as the Flute Concerto in G and the Sinfonia Concertante. Another indication of maturing style is the growing freedom and ingenuity with which he radically reshapes the themes at their returns, even, as in K417, the opening subject of the tutti at its first restatement by the solo. (We find this trait in the nearly contemporary Quintet for Horn and Strings, also intended for Leutgeb, and the three Piano Concertos K413/387a, 414/385b, 415/387b.) In K417 there is, too, more variety of thematic material, especially in the first movement. Most striking, perhaps, is the rich chain of modulations at the end of the development, so often the place for the happiest play of Mozart's tonal fancy. Here, from the close of the second subject repeated in the dominant, the solo moves with new melodies through a bitter-sweet chain of B flat minor, D flat major, E flat minor and F minor to the dominant of C minor and the recapitulation. Technically, the movement made new demands on Leutgeb's powers, especially in the highest octave, where the solo ascends thrice to the sixteenth partial.

In the Andante, a kind of dreamy romanza in B flat, Mozart gives the solo smooth, taxing downward leaps of octaves and tenths, all poised over breaks in the murmur of the strings. It is as if the player becomes a singer caught in a sudden spotlight on a

Ex.24

stage. Formally, the movement falls into three thematic sequences, with a prelude of ten bars. In each, Mozart arranges the material differently and makes each one a little shorter than the last. The Rondo (lacking, unusually, any qualifying indication) is pure delight, again testing the soloist severely, especially in the last fifteen accelerated bars marked 'più allegro'. Here soloist and orchestra make great play with a short, galloping figure of repeated semi-quavers (played under and in alternation with the refrain theme) which was heard earlier as an appendage to the solo's second entry. Indeed, Mozart's delicate use of this little figure throughout the Rondo gives it something of the quality of his chamber music.

Equally poetic is his treatment of a subsidiary theme, basically in C minor, in the second episode:

Ex.25

The violin figure chirrups along, at varying pitch, sharply contrasted with sustained, sonorous calls on the horn.

The third concerto, K447, is another controversial work. Some critics have denied that Mozart wrote it for Leutgeb, but this point at least can be settled beyond dispute by examination of the autograph (which admittedly for some time was not publicly available). Mozart wrote his friend's name at two pause-marks in the last movement. But the date '1783', at the side of the first page, is not in Mozart's hand, and some scholars have argued on grounds of style, especially the rich scoring for clarinets and bassoons (instead of oboes and *ripieno* horns), that this concerto is a late work composed at some time between *Don Giovanni* and *Così fan tutte*. Against this rather tenuous theory stands the fact that Mozart did not enter this concerto in his thematic catalogue. While there are a score or so of post-1784 compositions not entered, they are mostly either minor works or else the reasons for their omission are obvious. No major work, such as K447, is omitted, and it is almost inconceivable that Mozart could just have forgotten all about it if he did compose it after February 1784. But there remains the curious fact that he himself gave the sheets of the autograph two sequences of numbering, one for the first movement and a second for the last two movements together. This is quite exceptional, and might suggest that he wrote the three movements at two different times, and so might have left the 'concerto' out of his catalogue as not being a unified work. But on the whole, it seems safer to accept a date between November 1783 and late February 1784 as being most likely. After all, there is no reason why he should not have composed two concertos for Leutgeb in fairly quick succession.

The play of Mozart's musical fancy is richer in this first movement – simply marked 'Allegro' – than in any of the previous horn concertos. Though thematically quite compact, the music combines not a little of the quality of the piano concertos written in the spring of 1784 with some of the sinewy rhythms of, say, the 'Linz' symphony. The strings alone quietly announce the first phrase of the principal subject, the second phrase of which is played *forte* by the full orchestra, in strongly chromatic harmony with the wind doubling the strings. Similarly, the melting second subject (different only in phrasing from a subsidiary theme in the first movement of the Piano Concerto K467) merges into the *forte* of a vigorous, leaping string passage which leads to the codetta with its whimsical, graceful ending. The soloist repeats the first subject, and extends it. A transition leads to the second subject, now in the dominant, and the solo takes it up, supported by mounting excitement on the strings. After a brief allusion to the first subject, the codetta is heard again, in a magical shift to D flat major. In this warm, romantic key, a new melody for the soloist introduces a noble passage which culminates in a lovely enharmonic modulation on the horn itself:

Ex.26

Then, through a sequence of modulations (D minor, B flat, C minor, and G major), sumptuous by the standard of any of Mozart's mature developments, the music flows quietly back to the recapitulation. This is marked by some nice abbreviation and rearrangement of the material. Throughout, there is a closer integration of the solo horn with the orchestra than in any earlier concerto, and it is partly this which makes the movement so satisfying.

The autograph of the second movement is headed with the words 'Romance. Di Wolfgang Amadeo Mozart'. No other slow movement bears such an inscription, which has a fortuitous significance. Now for the first and only time in these concertos Mozart turned to A flat, a key which he favoured for barely a dozen movements in all his instrumental music. But his use of it was remarkably consistent. Here, as for instance in the Andante of the slightly earlier E flat String Quartet, the harmony is exceptionally rich, and the mood seems deeply reflective. Formally, this Romance is a rondo of a simple though rather old-fashioned cast, in the manner of C. P. E. Bach. There are four returns of the main theme which, in all, takes up half of the movement. (Mozart used a somewhat similar style in the Rondo in D for Piano, K485.) The solo itself announces the theme, whose carefully balanced simplicity has something of the 'moulded form' of the slow movement of the later piano concertos. The episodes mostly revert to E flat, and are enlivened by a short rising demisemidemiquaver figure, not unlike some of the figuration in the first movement. It is a point of some interest that the solo part of this Romance is almost identical with that of a Romance for Horn and Strings by Michael Haydn, which is first known from a catalogue of about 1795 and which was published in c. 1805. The resemblance is so close that it cannot be accidental. Though we know nothing at all of the circumstances, it seems on the whole more likely that Mozart was the originator, and Michael Haydn the borrower. Mozart's own definite statement on his autograph lends colour to this idea.

The clear-cut rondo sparkles with the spirit of 'la chasse' – bounding rhythms and fluent melody alternating with true horn-calls, all fashioned into a most satisfying whole. The wealth of humour, sonority (especially the delicate touches from the woodwind) and inventiveness is astonishing, even for Mozart, in a movement which barely exceeds 200 bars. His skill in reshaping the links between the rondo theme and the two episodes, at their several returns, gives continual pleasure. The texture is light, for he uses the lower strings sparingly. Though his demands on Leutgeb's technique are pitched rather lower than in the finales of the previous concertos and in that of the one yet to come, the style is more artistic. For the solo is as fully integrated with the orchestra as its nature allows. Take, for instance, the passage (near the end of the movement) which is a modified return of the first episode (Ex 27, overleaf). Here the new horn-call blends perfectly with the rhythmical figure on the strings. In the second episode, which is heard but once, Mozart springs a delightful surprise. He introduces as its theme the principal melody of the Romance, in its own key of A flat but with the notes adapted to the bustle of 6/8 time–a witty piece of self-quotation which almost amounts to parody.

Mozart completed his last Horn Concerto, K495, on 26 June 1786, barely two months after *Le Nozze di Figaro*, and entered it in his thematic catalogue with a laconic remark in German, 'for

Ex.27

Leutgeb'. The autograph has survived in a sadly fragmentary state, only six leaves out of the original twenty-three. The text has therefore to be supplemented from the first edition and later MS copies: in current editions it is inconsistent and not entirely satisfactory, but not so as materially to affect a discussion of the music. The extant leaves of the autograph are something of a curiosity, being written in blue, green, red and black ink. This has generally been taken as another form of Mozart's expression of jocularity towards Leutgeb, whom the colours were intended to confuse. But this assumes that the latter played from the autograph, which is most unlikely. Moreover, in the autograph of the very next work which Mozart wrote (the Piano Trio in G, K496, completed a fortnight later), he used black and red ink, with no obvious ulterior motive.

In K495 Mozart preferred the horns and oboes used in K417 to the clarinets and bassoons of K447. Melodically, the first two movements of K495 show some striking affinities to works written not long before or immediately afterwards. The opening of the Allegro is very similar to that of 'Die Maurerfreude', K471; its third subject is underlaid by a fluttering figure on the strings almost identical in pattern to the beginning of the overture to *Figaro*. The Romanza opens with a melody which is practically the same as the first theme of the Andante of the Duet Sonata K497 (and in the same key), and the middle episode clearly echoes the opening of the

G minor Piano Quartet. Such affinities combine to lend weight and seriousness to these two movements, which continue the excellence of K447 on a higher plane. A curious feature of the work is that in most of the tuttis of its first and last movements the solo horn plays in unison with the first of the two *ripieno* horns. Why Mozart adopted this rather old-fashioned practice here and not in K417 (the only other similarly scored) remains a mystery. What is clear is that the solo part of K495 marks a further advance in technical difficulty, especially with some high-lying cantabile passages, with rapid runs and the use of successions of stopped notes. One wonders if Leutgeb had asked Mozart for a new challenge.

The opening theme is bold and spacious, quite different in character from that in any previous horn concerto, and more sharply contrasted with the dulcet second subject. Mozart treats the latter rather less interestingly than a third melody, which he gives first to the strings, then to the oboe supported by the solo horn above the Figaroesque flutterings on the strings (see Ex. 28, overleaf). This rises to a splendid climax before the solo enters with a much simplified outline of the opening subject. Very economically, Mozart builds up the music towards the development, which he launches with a short, vivid operatic gesture just before the re-entry of the modified opening theme, in C minor, and then expands it through an exciting sequence of remote keys. In the recapitulation, Mozart selects, modifies and regroups his material with great ingenuity. The coda is based largely on Ex. 28.

The slow movement ('Andante') is yet another Romanza. (Why did Mozart use this term more often in these horn concertos than in any other instrumental group ? Was he perhaps following a tradition established by Rössler, in many of whose horn concertos the slow movements bear this marking ?) Blending lyrical warmth with veiled intimacy, the music surpassed in variety and depth even the lovely Romance of K447. The sixteen bars or so of the first episode, where the solo enters in F, are a marvellous example of 'il filo' – the natural thread of a compact melody spun over the carefully spaced patterns of the strings. The second episode, in G minor, provides a vigorous, wider-ranging contrast. For the coda, Mozart devised an exquisite little dialogue between the strings and the soloist, over a long pedal on basses and horns, replacing the latter by the oboes in the penultimate bars – so simple yet so moving.

The rondo ('Allegro vivace' – the sole use of this marking in

Ex.28

these concertos) opens with the catchy refrain theme in Mozart's happiest 'galloping' vein. He makes great play with the contrast between this and the more compact subsidiary melodies. As before, the most exciting music comes in the second episode, where this new tune (Ex. 29), in C minor, enters over some splendidly varied string writing, and modulates through A flat, G minor and F minor to a cleverly foreshadowed return of the refrain theme, sharply pointed by haunting notes on the horn. Later, after the cadenza, the refrain theme passes through some new chromatic modification and

Ex.29

extension before its final restatement in the coda, which, as in the Romanza, ends with a delightful dialogue between soloist and strings.

Whether or not Leutgeb really was as simple as Mozart's inscriptions suggest, the purely musical personality which comes out in this sequence of horn concertos is remarkable. The wonderful cantilena of the solo parts lingers gratefully in the memory, like the utterance of a dignified yet witty conversationalist, at ease among friends. Mozart has transmuted the spirit of the chase into the mellow discourse of an instrumental *Capriccio*.

The Clarinet Concerto

After finishing his last horn concerto, Mozart wrote only three more concertos during the next five years. They were all for piano. By the autumn of 1788, when he had finished the three last symphonies and the great String Trio, he was overtaken by creative and physical exhaustion, which lasted until the end of 1789. The tale of this sad decline has been told often enough, and need not be repeated here. It is more important to realise that his last concerto, the incomparable work for clarinet, is not an isolated phenomenon, but is part of the revival of his powers which began, slowly at first, with the production of *Così fan tutte* early in 1790, and gathered pace in the last fifteen months of his life. In timbre and renewal of spirit, the Clarinet Concerto has much in common with the other master-pieces which he wrote in 1791. Unfortunately we do not know its exact date, because (as with a number of other compositions of his last years) he entered it in his catalogue without month or day, and with the simple statement: 'A Concerto for clarinet for the elder Herr Stadler. Instrumentation: 2 violins, viola, 2 bassoons, two horns and basses.' But the concerto follows the March of the Priests and the overture to *Die Zauberflöte* (28 September) and precedes the little Masonic Cantata (15 November). Within these limits we can fix a more precise date because, fortunately, on 7 October Mozart wrote to his wife saying that having ordered some black coffee, and after smoking 'a splendid pipe of tobacco', he 'orchestrated almost the whole of Stadler's rondo'. This suggests that he finished the entire work well before the middle of the month.

The very gifted recipient of this masterpiece was Anton Stadler (1753–1812) who had been living in Vienna, with other members of his musical family, some ten years before Mozart settled there. Anton and his brother Johann probably took the clarinet parts in early performances of the Wind Serenade, K361. Like Mozart, Anton Stadler was a Freemason, and became one of his close friends in the later 1780s. By all accounts, his technique was pheno-menal: but it was probably his deeply expressive powers which inspired Mozart to compose some fine works for him, including, besides the concerto, the equally lovely Quintet K581, and the clarinet part in the Trio for Viola, Clarinet and Piano K498. Famous also as a basset-horn player, Stadler caused a sensation in Prague by his rendering of the obbligato part in 'Non più di fiori' at the early performances of *La Clemenza di Tito*. He thus ranks with Leutgeb and Brunetti as one of the most influential and inspiring soloists in the whole span of Mozart's concerto-writing. The clarinet on which Stadler played this concerto was an uncommon type of instrument, recently named the 'basset-clarinet'. Its compass is directly related to that of the music and to its curious history.

The concerto began its life, probably early in 1791, as the first movement of a work for basset-horn, strings, two flutes and two horns, in G major. The autograph sketch runs to 199 bars; at bar 180, Mozart changed the key to A major, and had clearly begun to turn the piece into a clarinet concerto. He reworked the music of this extensive sketch, with few major changes, as the first movement of K622. But it is the crowning irony that Mozart's final masterpiece in concerto form should have come down to us in a defective form because he wrote it for a special type of clarinet which quickly became obsolete.

Recent research has shown that this instrument, devised by Stadler in collaboration with the court instrument-maker Theodor Lotz, had additional keys which added four semitones below the lowest note (E) of the soprano clarinet in A. The evidence for this is in the current text of the music based (because the autograph is lost) on the earliest editions, all of about 1801. In many passages of the solo part, especially those in semiquavers and demisemi-quavers in the lowest register, we now rarely hear the music as Mozart wrote it. The solo duplicates or imitates other parts, or crosses them, in a way quite alien to his normally skilful and sensi-tive writing for solo instruments in his maturity. These changes were probably made in André's publishing house, to adapt Mozart's music to the normal, widely used clarinet in A, after Stadler's 'basset-clarinet' lost its attraction for soloists.[1]

This concerto is one of Mozart's most marvellous scores. Melodically, it has the smooth, easy flow characteristic of his mature works in A, such as the Piano Concerto K488. Some of the themes sound like a recreation of parts of the Clarinet Quintet. Here and there we hear echoes of *Die Zauberflöte* which add solem-nity to grace. There are few really sharp contrasts in the scoring. The clarinet's own sensuous warmth is matched by the orchestra-tion which, lacking oboes, produces a wonderfully mellow sound, with a luminous texture of shifting light and shade heightened by a fluid sense of key. Yet the music is also cohesive and strong, partly because of the frequent use of canonic devices. By exploiting the clarinet's agility and varied tone-colour, Mozart creates a new standard of virtuosity, but always as part of an integrated artistic whole (even as he had done in his Bassoon Concerto, on a smaller scale), and never allows the brilliance of the instrument to become an end in itself, as did Weber.

[1] The edition of K622, by Alan Hacker (Schott, 1974), for basset-clarinet and piano, is the first publication of an attempted reconstruction of the original clarinet line. The Eulenberg score, no. 778, was reissued (1971) with a foreword by Hacker and his 'suggestions for the restoration of Mozart's clarinet part'. The volume of the *Neue Mozart Ausgabe* devoted to the clarinet concerto (1977) contains, besides the traditional text, a reconstructed version for basset-clarinet.

The easy-paced Allegro, one of Mozart's most poetic inspirations, is spaciously constructed, with great inner strength. From its exquisite lyrical opening, the tutti builds up, with forceful prolongation of phrases, to a chordal climax on the dominant. But then, instead of the expected new theme, Mozart beguiles us with a modified version of the opening subject stated in canon:

Ex.30

and leading to the same climax as before. Only at this point does the clarinet (having strengthened the first violins in the ritornello) enter as a solo instrument. It decorates and expands the first subject with a brief flourish of its whole repertoire of expressiveness – brilliant passage-work, arpeggios, and wide leaps. A short tutti leads to another, very haunting subject in two sections, the first in A minor, the second in C major:

Ex.31

The whole passage, accompanied by strings alone, is strongly reminiscent of parts of the Clarinet Quintet in mood and texture. Brusquely, the tutti shifts the tonality to E major for the second subject proper, and this also is cast in two extended sections, the latter veering towards F sharp minor and a pause. Then the solo's canonic first entry reappears, succeeded by a remarkable passage in which the solo provides an Alberti bass to a passage of tight imitation in the violins with a figure derived from the opening tutti. This bass dissolves into airy arpeggios, and the exposition closes with bustling material, again from the tutti.

The development begins with a short restatement of the first subject (drastically modified) in the dominant, passes in scale passages through C sharp minor, and returns to Ex. 31, first in D major, then modulating to F sharp minor. Here Mozart raises the music to a different, almost eerie plane with an extraordinary orchestral section, first in F sharp minor, then repeated in D minor: it is as if a shadow of desolation passes over the music, heightened by the effect of woodwind and strings playing in octave unison:

A short return of vigorous passage-work from the ritornello, slightly expanded, ceases abruptly on an unaccompanied rising scale for the solo which leads, most beautifully, to the recapitulation. This, being some seventy bars shorter than the exposition, offers a striking essay in refinement and concentration. Mozart leaves the tonic much less frequently and introduces subtle modifications in the phrase endings. It is as if he were showing us a familiar landscape from a point of new perspective.

The Adagio, in D, is music of utter simplicity, which seems to reflect the timeless and beatific vision of a mind at peace with itself. In parts, it echoes both the motet 'Ave verum corpus' and *Die Zauberflöte*. Except for a short middle section in A, the music hardly leaves the tonic. But, as often, Mozart's invention is heard at its best within a restricted framework. In the second section of the reprise he elaborates the bassoon parts, but simplifies those for the horns, and alters the melodic line of the upper strings so that the whole passage sounds enriched and totally fresh.

In the finale, an elaborate rondo in 6/8, the solo line soars, swoops and hovers as do few others in any Mozart concertos. (It recalls the brilliant finale of the Piano Sonata in F, K332/300k.) Most of the melodies are pure 'linked sweetness long drawn out', with delightfully unpredictable phrase lengths, which also help to make the bravura passages so fascinating and an integral part of the whole design. The main subject

Ex.33

combines a slight hesitancy with a varied pace, features which Mozart alters slightly at each of the three returns. After keeping steadily in the tonic to develop Ex. 33 and two subsidiary themes, he tinges the rather mournful second subject with a haze of shifting tonality:

Ex.34

but steers the music towards the dominant. Two new melodies, in F sharp minor and in D major, introduce the haunting central episode which is built round a culmination of Ex. 34, treated in an arresting passage of musical aposiopesis:

Ex.35

– a device used, for instance, with great effect in the finale of his last quartet, and wholly characteristic of his late style. Whatever emotional interpretation one puts on this music, perhaps equating the technical hesitance with momentary self-doubt, this brilliantly effective passage marks one of the climaxes of Mozart's mastery as a concerto writer. Immediately after it, the soloist strides out from the shadows with a leap of nearly two octaves, and whirls the music, on the wings of brilliant passage-work, into the recapitulation, so rich in the variety, the sinuous grace and iridescent harmony that colour the whole concerto.

While much of this work may seem to be suffused with sadness, it is not more or less so than many others that Mozart wrote in the preceding five years. This concerto has often been described as 'autumnal', but there is no reason to regard this quality, whatever the adjective may mean in terms of instrumental music, as evidence of a foreboding of imminent death. But the Clarinet Concerto certainly offers us the final paradox of Mozart's career – music for public performance which is also one of his most withdrawn and intimate masterpieces.

In less than two months after finishing it he was dead, leaving the Requiem as a torso to puzzle posterity. It was surely a fitting crown to his career that his last instrumental work should have been a concerto, and that, too, for the wind instrument which since his youth he had loved above all others.

Index of Main Works